Warri

Victory on the

Battlefront of the Mind

Edited and Compiled By

Judith Victoria Hensley

Warrior Women, Victory on the Battlefront of the Mind

Compiled and Edited by
Judith Victoria Hensley

ISBN-13:
978-1986708326

ISBN-10:
1986708322

Printed by Create Space, an Amazon.com Company CreateSpace, Charleston, SC

www.CreateSpace.com/TITLEID

Available from Amazon.com, CreateSpace.com, and other retail outlets

Cover Design by Judith Victoria Hensley

Cover Subject: Judy Saylor Hensley

Dedication

For the warrior women who are still fighting the good fight.

Thank You

To each woman who took time and had the courage to share her unique story in this book.

To each woman who allowed me to do a photoshoot with them for this project.

Message from the Author

The Warrior Women Book Series was birthed after the first book, **Mother Warrior** was in print. There were so many stories that deserved to be told and documented, that no one volume could possibly hold them all.

The second book in the series is **Warrior Women, the Power of Prayer**, which features stories from women who saw circumstances in their lives change as a direct result of prayer.

The third book **Warrior Women, Healing the Brokenhearted** is dedicated to stories from women who have experience God's love and healing in the midst of heartache and loss.

This is the fourth book in the series, **Warrior Women, Victory on the Battlefront of the Mind** in which the writers share their struggles in decision making, seeking God's will, or health issues of loved ones. These women have also experienced victory through God's peace and intervention in their individual circumstances.

If you have a story to share, you may contact me on my Facebook page: Judith Victoria Hensley, Author

Table of Contents

*Note: Not all women who contributed a story appear in the photo gallery. A photo of each author who did participate in a photo shoot appears at the end of her own story.

The LORD lift up His countenance upon thee, and give thee peace. (Numbers 6:26 King James Version)

Peace I leave with you, my peace I give unto you: not as the world giveth, give I unto you. Let not your heart be troubled, neither let it be afraid. *(John 14:27)*

Thou wilt keep him in perfect peace, whose mind is
stayed on thee: because he trusteth in thee." (Isaiah
26:3)

Not Good Enough
Judith Victoria Hensley

Each one of us has a life experience that is uniquely our own, although there may be similarities with other people's journeys. The things we have gone through or are going through in this life will prejudice us in the ways we look at and interpret every day events.

Forty years after a divorce, I still struggle with self-esteem. Divorce wasn't supposed to happen to me. I was a church girl who grew up in a Christian home. My dad became a pastor when I was a young adult. I desperately wanted God's will to be done in my life.

I was the girl everyone thought would marry a minister, a preacher, an evangelist, or a missionary. Everyone thought they knew the path that was before me. I thought they were right. My greatest desire was to serve God beside a man that had answered God's call on his life and we would share the work together.

Several guys had been interested in me. A few had said they knew it was God's will that we get married, but God did not speak to me about any of those young men, even though they were Christians. When I did fall in love and the proposal came, I was still seeking God's direction. I fasted, prayed, placed fleeces before the Lord. The answers to those prayers and the circumstances that would allow us to marry at the end of our junior year in college all came together, and I truly believed I was following God's direction.

There was never a time that I didn't want God's blessings or want to follow His master plan for my life. I was positive divorce was not part of that plan. The possibility never crossed my mind.

My husband and I worked in church together, sang and played guitar in church, directed children's church, and discussed the possibility of Medical Missions when he finished school. We never fought. We were united in our love for the great outdoors. I was clueless that other forces and temptations beyond our marriage were at work on his end.

How could things go so wrong? After the divorce I went back to college, taking my 15-month old son with me, while I earned and added a teaching certification to my degree. My self-esteem couldn't have been any lower. I felt so wounded and hideous that I thought people only spoke to me out of pity. I was so damaged on the inside that I felt like on the outside I was scarred similar to a burn victim. My whole world was upside down and I had not been prepared in any way for the possibility of what happened. In my life and in my family, I was convinced that as a dedicated Christian such an event could never happen – and especially not to me.

So, I came under a wounded mindset of "not good enough." The man I loved, my husband, the man who was the father of my child found me "not good enough." I let that carry over into every other aspect of my life and image of myself. I wanted to die, literally. I felt as if I had been cursed in a way that I could never be loved again, and that no matter how hard I tried, I would never be enough.

Forty years ago, the church didn't place divorced women in any kind of active ministry roles. Divorce equated failure. Some even told me that it was a shame that I had missed God's will for my life. Statements like these left slashing injuries on top of the wounds that were still trying to heal.

I knew there were people who constantly judged me through a lens of "failure." I let that yardstick cripple me, without realizing that God never viewed me in that way.

I wanted to be invisible. Invisible was safe. At the same time, I was determined to remain faithful to God. I never stopped wanting God's divine purpose to be accomplished in my life. Even inside of church circles I felt like I was on the outside looking in on a place of love and acceptance that was never going to be available to me. I was an outsider, left out of the joys of marriage, left out of the covering of a husband, left out of leadership positions or ministry possibilities as a single woman, divorced, and with a small child.

In Nathaniel Hawthorne's novel, *The Scarlet Letter*, Hester Prynn had to wear a scarlet letter "A" to mark her and shame her before the community. I felt very much like Hester, but my scarlet letter was a "D" for Divorced.

I had sung in church settings since high school. With my guitar and long straight hair I had traveled from place to place with our church or with our college choir singing about Jesus. It got me labeled as a hippie Jesus chick. I loved to sing, but the thoughts of singing or being the center of attention in front of a congregation again was a battlefront on which the enemy had an upper hand in my mindas.

"How can you stand up in front of people and sing about the love of God after all that has happened to you? Your life is a failure. People don't want to see or hear a divorced woman up in front of the church," the tormentor whispered. The deceiver knew my weak spot and took full advantage of my wounded state.

I let those lies silence me for years. I sang at home. I sang in the car. I sang from the church pew. Eventually, I was asked to be part of a church praise and worship team, which I gladly did for many years.

I taught Sunday School. I had led a teen Bible study in my home. I was allowed to fill those roles.

Still, I believed there was a call on my life in a different direction, but I wasn't sure what it was. Over twenty years ago, I was asked to write a weekly newspaper column in our local paper that began with a trip our church had taken to the famous Brownsville Revival in Pensacola, Florida. God threw a door open for me there and gave me the courage to walk through. I had been writing since third grade, when my first column appeared in the *King Arthur's Court* page of the *Chicago Heights Star* in Chicago Heights, Illinois.

Writing was something I loved. It was a place where my imagination could take wings.

Over my teaching career, together with my students, we produced and published eleven *Foxfire*-type book projects. Six were in a very primitive magazine format and five were bound as regular books fit for library shelves. I didn't realize that in helping the students become story gatherers and writers, I was developing my own love for the gathering process and learning how to put a book together.

I attempted what seemed like the impossible because I was doing it for them, for family, and friends in the community. It was an incredible teaching opportunity as a Language Arts instructor, and a way of allowing people's stories (which would have otherwise been lost) to be recorded and documented in the pages of real books. Student initiated, community based, hands-on learning was hard work, but resulted in great joy for the students, their families, and for me.

I was overjoyed when my own first book, *Sir Thomas the Eggslayer* was picked up by a publisher, followed by *Terrible Tina*, and then *Mountain Wisdom: Mountain Folk*. I had found a silent, invisible place to do something productive outside my classroom and follow a childhood dream of becoming a writer. Even then, I wanted to call myself a writer in my mind, but I just couldn't accept that description of myself. It felt like I was a fraud. In my mind, I was still only a writer "wanna be."

But I continued to write. Writing a weekly newspaper column was good discipline in the school of writing. There is always a deadline and a certain amount of space to fill. Finding a new topic each week is a challenge but has kept me always thinking ahead to the next column I need to write. I've written well over a thousand newspaper columns in all these years. I don't know my newspaper columns have impacted the lives of others, but they have certainly impacted mine. It has been an opportunity to be faithful in the little things.

When I felt the Holy Spirit nudge me to open an author's page on Facebook, I was shocked to realize that I had either compiled, written, or contributed to over thirty books, plus numerous magazine articles, and my weekly newspaper column. I was truly surprised. I had not been keeping count. No matter what I wrote or how much I wrote, I always had the feeling that someone else could do it better.

I distinctly heard the Holy Spirit speak to me about this surprising revelation. "This was all practice. This was a learning curve for you."

In some incredible way, I passed from the "wanna be" writer to realizing that in God's capacity, I had become a writer without ever being able to acknowledge it as part of my purpose and destiny. I could honestly say that I was not only a writer, but an author! I had been writing since I was a child, but it always seemed my dream was just out of reach.

It is only by the grace of God that I never gave up. I've written in many genres from children's middle school chapter books, Appalachian culture, Christian encouragement, and one Christian romance novel. Even so, it seemed like I was not doing God's work as much as I wanted.

Most recently, God has called me to compile women's stories for the *Warrior Women Series*. It is God's call and my privilege of opening a door for women to share their faith, trials, and the amazing power of God's love in their lives. These books are an opportunity for other women of faith who have felt personal inadequacies in life, their own "not good enough" experiences, to have a voice and encourage other women and urge them on to victory.

The stories gathered for the *Warrior Women Series* are evidence that every trial, every heartache, every difficult situation we walk through in this life becomes a filter of how we perceive ourselves and other events in life. However, those things also become an opportunity for personal growth, increased faith, awareness of God's great love, and empower us to reach out to other women who are walking similar paths.

In God's hands, nothing is wasted. No hurt is unhealable. No disappointment is insurmountable. No failure is unredeemable. There is no hole so black that God's light won't dispel the darkness. There is no wound so deep that God can't bring it to the surface and make it whole again.

The battles we fight in our minds are often our greatest ones. Broken bones mend. Bruises disappear. Scars soften and discoloration fades. But words, accusations, and self-doubt bounce around in our heads for years and influence our perception of the world around us.

If we get overlooked or passed over for legitimate reasons, it may still feel like rejection. If the people we look up to don't ever say an encouraging word or do anything to validate our hard work, it may resurrect those feelings of "not good enough." If those in ministry don't view our calling as important, we may translate that disappointment to a perception of God's view of our work. If we aren't invited into the inner circle of the "popular ones," we may be tempted to feel like outcasts.

It can be a tricky and deceitful business. If we hunger after man's approval as we pursue God, we will do one of two things: 1) We can starve to death for lack of support and encouragement from those we esteem. 2) We can get so addicted to man's approval that we desire it more than we truly desire to please God.

I recently paid a visit to the Billy Graham Memorial Library. His life and calling over decades can be found throughout the tour. God's love spoke to me in so many ways as we walked through the halls and videos of a life well spent.

God doesn't call the most beautiful. He doesn't reserve powerful destinies for the most brilliant or the wealthiest. God calls ordinary people to do extraordinary things. Billy Graham's life is a testament to that fact.

The truth is, I am NOT good enough. None of us are good enough on our own. My efforts will never be enough. If we could have fulfilled the requirements of "good enough" on our own, Christ would never have had to become the sacrifice for our sins. We are complete in Jesus Christ. He is good enough. He can do the incredible in the lives of ordinary men and women.

Single and celibate for almost forty years, I believe God has protected me and sheltered me during that time and set me apart to draw close to Him in a way that I would not have been able to do if I was totally devoted to a husband and filling the role I believed was required as wife and mother. Having acknowledged this, I still believe that God has a sense of humor and can surprise us when we least expect it. I have learned to trust God with every aspect of my life.

I've experienced the goodness of God in thousands of ways since then, every single day of my life. There are times when we are wallowing in our pain that we become blinded to the provision and goodness of God toward us. His mercy and His grace have been more than sufficient for me. His love is everlasting toward me, and His faithfulness to me unquestionable. Yet, that overwhelming feeling of "not good enough" stuck with me for many years.

When we surrender all that we are to His hands and ask Him to shape us and mold us as He will into useful vessels, He will make some of clay, some of stone, some of glass, and others of silver and gold. How He raises us up to serve Him correlates to the place He has called us to serve.

He equips us to do what He has destined us to become. He trains us through our life experiences to have an understanding, compassion, and a testimony to others in that same place where we have been to have hope in Him. He provides the tools we need to accomplish the task we have been given. He teaches us the lessons we need to learn.

He sees our heart, our motives, our willingness, our obedience, and our love for Him. He delights in us as we learn to delight in Him.

He takes these wounded and broken dreamers that we are and recreates us in His image. And that, dear ones, will always be enough.

Judith Victoria Hensley

These things I have spoken unto you, that in me ye might have peace. In the world ye shall have tribulation: but be of good cheer; I have overcome the world. (John 16:33)

Be anxious for nothing, but in everything by prayer and supplication, with thanksgiving, let your requests be made known to God; and the peace of God, which surpasses all understanding, will guard your hearts and minds through Christ Jesus. (Philippians 4:6-7)

In One Minute, Your Whole Life Can Change

By Juanita Lee

I was on my way to the doctor for a check-up in 2011 and was nervous because I don't like going to the doctor for anything. My mother went with me to keep me company on the drive.

As the doctor was giving me the physical, I got the shock of my life. She turned to me and said, "Juanita, you have cancer. You need to go to Lexington."

Dumbfounded, I asked, "When?"

"Today. No later than tomorrow." She called and made arrangements for me to see someone the next day.

Just like that, I entered the world of cancer. In one minute, my whole life changed. In one minute, I was fighting for my life and fighting doubt, discouragement, and fear in my mind associated with the word "cancer."

I headed home and was thinking about my mother. My mind was troubled with what the future might hold for me and those I loved who depended on me.

"What am I going to tell her?" I didn't want to worry my mother any more than I had to.

I called my husband when I got back to work, then went to pick up my granddaughters from school. They have been in my care and I have raised them since they were babies. My precious girls, Sasha and Bobbie Jo – what was I going to tell them?

I kept it simple. I told them I was sick and needed to go to Lexington to see a doctor. I took the girls with me. I will never forget when we turned into the parking lot of the hospital.

Sasha said, "Why are we at the CANCER hospital?"

I almost broke down but was fighting with everything in me not to cry. I told the girls, "I have cancer." At that point, there was nothing else to tell until after I saw the doctor.

I met a doctor who said, "Someone likes you. I have had calls all day long from people wanting me to see you."

A biopsy was performed, and I was told that I was in second stage cervical cancer.

The doctor said, "Your number is 5. That means 5 chemo, 25 radiation, and 5 implants. The chemo and radiation will be in Corbin, but the implants are given in Lexington because they are complicated. They take up to five hours and you must be asleep."

The fear I was dealing with after this news was unspeakable. My mind was full of unanswered questions. "Lord, PLEASE help me," I begged.

I tried to remember and explain everything to Sasha, Bobbie Jo and the rest of my family exactly the way it had been told to me. I knew they would try to help me through it all.

Needless to say, the chemo was horrible. I got very sick with each of those treatments. They took five hours to get, also. I would get very, very weak after 24 hours. They always gave them to me on Friday. By Monday it was time for another radiation.

Treatments were five days a week. On my last implant, I was thanking God that it was the last one. I will never forget sitting in that room getting ready for it.

I could hear the pinging of a tool. They measure each person because the bed is fixed just for the individual. It always made me so nervous! I knew that if I wanted to live, I had to make myself do what the doctors had said.

I had started talking to a nurse during these procedures. She was kind of stand-offish with me, but I learned her name. She was kind of tough but to the point. There was another nurse who was always with her. She was with me every time, even in surgery.

They informed me that they would not put anything in my mouth unless I had trouble breathing. I had been there four times previously for treatment and had never had any previous breathing complications. That time was different.

I was being put in the bed to have the surgery for the last implant. My face felt numb. I said, "Loretta, something is WRONG!" Fear tried to overwhelm my thoughts. I had come so far and was at the end of my treatments, but I knew something was wrong.

I turned my head to the side to look for my nurse and was certainly not expecting what I saw! There was a huge angel standing there! From his appearance he was a warrior angel, standing there looking down at me.

As I looked at him, I was no longer afraid. I knew he was there for a reason, but I didn't know what exactly. I did know that he was there for my sake because I felt such great peace.

I didn't tell the doctors what I saw. I just looked at the amazing angel as they put me to sleep. My mind was fixed on him instead of the fear which had tried to come in.

I had a tube down my throat to help me breathe and they were removing it as I was waking up. I knew then why the angel was there. He had been sent to make war with the enemy for my life. I know the Lord sent an angel to keep me from death.

I kept this all to myself on the way home. I never wanted to worry my family. I faced cancer and I faced death, but not by myself. I was comforted to know the Lord had sent an angel to take care of me.

I have been cancer free for seven years and I know I owe it all to Jesus who said, "I will never leave you or forsake you."

I have fought many battles since then, but I know when we REALLY need the Lord, He will be right there, and right on time. I have this confidence in part because when I needed it most, He sent an angel to stand watch over me and rescue me from the hands of death.

I trust His Word. "We know that all things work together for good to them that love God, to them who are the called according to his purpose." (Romans 8:28)

Juanita Lee

He hath delivered my soul in peace from the battle that was against me: for there were many with me. (Psalm 55:18)

And I will give peace in the land, and ye shall lie down, and none shall make you afraid: and I will rid evil beasts out of the land, neither shall the sword go through your land. (Leviticus 26:6)

Beyond the White Horse
Karen Rode

I spent many years of my Christian life living as a Pharisee, desperate to look holy both to myself and to others. So strong was this desire it was difficult for me to accept Christ as Savior because that meant acknowledging I was a sinner.

As one preacher observed, "We come to Jesus confessing that we are sinners in need of a Savior, then spend the rest of our lives trying to convince ourselves and everyone else we're not really that bad after all."

John Fischer's description of the life of a Pharisee is described in a humorous but painfully accurate allegory in his book, *Dark Horse: The Story of a Winner*. The desire to be "holy, righteous, Christian" is represented by white spots on a horse's coat.

For as long as I could remember, I had always wanted to be a white horse. I wasn't all white, but my good ancestry had left me with more white than most horses I knew, and fortunately, in the most important places. Most of my face was white, and the white of my front leg ran up to my shoulder so that if I stood at an angle...with my good leg out...and my head slightly cocked...all you could see was white.

...I was sent to a special ranch where they trained horses like me to think, walk, and prance like white horses...We learned how to pose so as to show the most amount of white (without looking unnatural). – John Fischer

My desire for holiness, whiteness, was real. My method for achieving it faulty. When faced inexorably with my sin, I simply tried harder to be white, to scrub myself cleaner, to pose more effectively. I joined a deliverance ministry, convinced that it would produce the perfection I so longed for. All it did was expose more of my sin and increase my frenzied Pharisaical efforts to be holy. I fasted; I prayed; I copied entire books of scripture; I listened to the

Bible on tape throughout the night; I isolated myself from social events.

All my efforts failed. God withstood me at every point while I wore myself out on the treadmill of self-effort. Finally, I repented. (Repentance means "to change your mind.")

I acknowledged the truth that I am a sinner with no redeeming qualities, no reason for God to love me. Creator God loves me simply because He made me and it's His nature to love. I came home as a prodigal, declaring, "I am not worthy to be called your child, make me as one of Your hired servants."

As the Word promises, the assimilation of that truth into my inner being transformed me (Rom. 12:2). No longer did I have to try to be good. I was free. I began to enjoy life at a whole new level. My goal was to obey God the best I knew how and leave all judgment of myself and others up to Him. I became like like Ruth of old, gleaning in the fields of the Lord while enjoying ever increasing communion with Him.

As believers we will forever be servants of our God and King. However, to those who choose to follow Jesus as disciples, He opens the door to a more intimate relationship.

"I no longer call you servants, because a servant does not know his master's business. Instead, I have called you friends, for everything that I learned from my Father I have made known to you." (John 15:15 New King James Version)

Scripture also refers to believers collectively as the bride of Christ. The Apostle Paul writes, "I am jealous for you with a godly jealousy. I promised you to one husband, to Christ, so that I might present you as a pure virgin to him." (2 Cor. 11:2)

Contented in the life I had built around the theology and experience of being a servant I was stunned when Jesus suddenly invaded my well-ordered existence. He challenged me to repent, to change my mind once again.

I seldom dream, which makes this God-given dream stand out in vivid detail. In my dream, I was dressed in casual clothes scurrying around, running in and out of an old, ornate, stone cathedral, preparing for a wedding. As maid-of-honor I was attending to last minute details for the bride. It was almost time for the wedding to begin. I ran to the room where I had left my dress to change my clothes. The dress was missing!

Frantic, I dashed outside to see if anyone knew what had happened to my dress. The organ was playing. The procession was imminent. Should I walk down the aisle in my street clothes? A bridesmaid appeared in an upper window and I lifted my arms, so she could pull me into the church. Someone came behind me, who I knew was a friend, put his arms around my waist and lifted me off the ground.

I protested, *"Don't pick me up! You'll hurt your back!"*

The friend set me down. I turned to face him and the presence of Christ shining out from his face, eyes and torso was so strong, so startling, so gripping that I was jolted awake, heart pounding, gasping for breath.

My immediate thought was, "God arrested me to prevent my falling off some kind of spiritual cliff." It took 20-30 minutes to calm my physiological reaction to this dream and several days before I had an inkling of its meaning.

Several weeks previously I had sensed that one season of my life was ending and another beginning. I did not realize how entrenched I was in walking familiar paths. My self-image as a sinner-servant had become a lifestyle, one with which I was comfortable, secure. I believe through the dream God was calling me to repent, change my mind about who I am.

The message was, *"Stop your frantic running around as a servant. You are not the maid-of-honor, you're the bride (of Christ). Take your position as such."*

I protested with typical arguments: "I'm not worthy, Lord. I'm not qualified to fill that role. I'm totally content where I am, living the life of a servant in the furthest reaches of Your kingdom." But, as in the past, my human reasonings fell to the ground in the face of God's call and I said, "Yes," to this new life, this new relationship with Jesus.

Necessity to walk in this new way came immediately. I received word that my brother was in the hospital diagnosed with a non-malignant tumor in the lining of his brain. Surgery was scheduled.

As a servant my knee-jerk mental reaction would have been to rush to prayer in fear begging God, "Please, please, please, DO something!" But I stopped, contemplating, "What would the wife of Christ do in this situation?"

I imagined myself in the kitchen with Jesus. How would I approach Him? First of all, with absolute trust, acknowledging that He had the best interests of my brother and his family in His mind and heart. There was to be no begging. I came to Him saying, "You know my heart's desire is for total and complete healing of my brother. But I trust You, my King, my Lord. No matter the outcome, I trust You. I know You will do what is best in this situation."

Then I waited. I waited two days until I felt released by the Spirit to contact friends and family to request prayer. (My brother's surgery was successful with the expectation of a full and complete recovery).

This position of bride is so new I have barely begun to explore the ramifications to my everyday life. And that's what it means to walk in the Spirit. To walk indicates movement, progress, new scenery, new experiences, new viewpoints.

The bride of Christ is part of the all things new described in the Bible.

"And I saw a new heaven and a new earth: for the first heaven and the first earth were passed away; and there was no more sea.

And I John saw the holy city, new Jerusalem, coming down from God out of heaven, prepared as a bride adorned for her husband.

And I heard a great voice out of heaven saying, Behold, the tabernacle of God is with men, and he will dwell with them, and they shall be his people, and God himself shall be with them, and be their God.

And God shall wipe away all tears from their eyes; and there shall be no more death, neither sorrow, nor crying, neither shall there be any more pain: for the former things are passed away.

And he that sat upon the throne said, Behold, I make all things new..." (Revelation 21:1-5)

"Occupy till I come." (Luke 19:13b)

Jesus exhorted in His parable of a nobleman traveling to a far country. What should we occupy? I propose we should occupy our position of blessing as the bride of Christ seated with Him in heavenly places. (Ephesians 1:3, 2:6) From that position we have access to the promises of Revelation 21. In God's presence we know God is our God and we are his children. The Father wipes away our tears and death has no sting. Sorrow, crying, and pain are no more. Not completely, not forever, but every woman whose testimony is written in this book has received those promises in measure. Through Christ we experience "all things new." We abide in a new reality, a new heaven and a new earth within ourselves.

Our future is a literal new heaven and new earth, a forever bliss. In the meantime, occupy till Jesus comes. Every day, in every situation, we can choose to occupy, hold fast our position in Him until He comes into that day, into that circumstance, wipes away our tears, heals the hurt, and shines His light into our darkness.

May the "pound" of faith, joy, love, patience He gave to us at salvation grow to ten pounds as in the parable and earn the commendation of our Nobleman, our King, our Husband. May He say to us, "Well, done."

Karen Rode

Then they made the plate of the holy crown of pure gold and wrote on it an inscription like the engraving of a signet: HOLINESS TO THE LORD. (Exodus 39:30)

I will both lie down in peace, and sleep; for You alone, O LORD, make me dwell in safety. (Psalm 4:8)

God is Still a Healer
Barb Saylor

My husband Ebb has always been a little on the wild side. Many people tend to be that way when they try to live life without a relationship with the Lord.

We both gave our hearts to God in 1978. He served the Lord for quite a while before he backslid and went back to his old ways. I was afraid of the consequences of his broken relationship with God because of the passage in Matthew 12:43-45 that warns of an unclean spirit returning to his host and bringing more evil ones with him. Ebb tried a few times to make things right with the Lord, but it seemed he could never quite get what he wanted or what he needed to help him hold on to his faith and avoid the old life.

My mind and heart were troubled because our house was divided on the spiritual level. I loved God, but I also loved my husband.

I struggled with thoughts about what I should do. Should I press on and serve God without my husband, or should I give up and quit also? Serving God without him by my side was going to be a battle. Only one person in a household serving God is a struggle for that person, if the unsaved spouse chooses to make it hard on them.

Jesus said that a house divided against itself cannot stand. (Mark 3:25)

I loved my husband. I loved God. I was torn. In my heart I wondered, "Can I do this? Can I continue to walk with God, serve Him, and attend church when my husband does not?"

As I pondered this over in my mind, my heart kept telling me, *"Yes! You can! The Lord will help you. You must hold on."*

It was in the late 80s and early 90s that he started getting sick. Ebb went to local doctors and was given medicine. He'd get better, but in a little while he would be sick again. He lost weight as well as physical strength.

He got to the place where he could barely get out of his chair. It seemed like he lived in the bathroom and couldn't go anywhere because his digestive system was so unhealthy.

I had been to sit with Ebb one night while he was in the hospital at Harlan, Kentucky, and had returned home. He called to talk to me about his condition. He was worried and so was I. I told him that he really needed to pray. He needed God's help. He knew he was in trouble.

As I lay there that night without my husband beside me in our bed, my heart was so heavy. My mind was filled with thoughts about our life together, his illness, and what the future would hold. I knew in my heart that if he didn't pray, he was going to die.

He wasn't praying so, I prayed. I begged God to have mercy on my husband one more time, and to send conviction because of His great mercy. Little did I know that God was already working in answer to my prayers.

The next night there was a man who came by his room in the hospital and asked permission to pray for him. This touched my husband's heart and he agreed for the man to pray for him and he prayed, also.

Ebb came home, but it wasn't long until he was so sick again that he could barely function. He decided to go to the VA Hospital. After that he prayed again.

It was as if the Lord was taking care of all the details for his care. He got a wonderful doctor who did everything she could to help him.

He was finally diagnosed with Chron's disease and placed on treatments every eight weeks. The treatments worked and gave him a life beyond his illness. With the treatments, his health returned, and he could eat anything he wanted, and go anywhere he wanted.

Ebb had his life back and did really well for a while. But, he turned away from the Lord again and went back to his old ways.

My mind was filled again with fears for my husband and concerns for the future. One day while we were working in the basement, we were fussing. I told him that if he wasn't careful the Lord was "going to get him."

His reply was, "I've been backslidden for four years and He hasn't got me yet!" As soon as those words came out of his mouth I knew, and he knew, he had said the wrong thing.

The enemy of our soul is always out to destroy us. He will use anything or anybody to try to get to us. As humans, most of us have some compassion and mercy on others, but we have to realize that the enemy of our soul does not have either. He has no love, no mercy, and no compassion.

There are times when we are doing well, and life is easy, then things change suddenly. We find ourselves in a battle zone, feeling so alone and as if there is no help and no hope.

There are times when we can't feel God's presence in our life. We can't even pray, and our peace is gone. Things begin to crumble, and our life feels like it's falling apart. It is in these times we are truly on the battlefront. Our weapons are prayer and the Word of God.

My life with Ebb had become like a war zone with me pulling one way, and him another. Slowly I watched the enemy pull him away from God and away from me, further and further.

I had been fasting and praying for the situation, but nothing seemed to be working. One night I went to church and my Spirit felt whipped. I was so discouraged and felt defeated.

I sat down by a lady in the church and said, "After all these years it looks like I'm not going to make it."

She started praying for me and the Holy Spirit came by and lifted my load. He restored my strength, and my hope returned. There was sweet peace overflowing my soul. My mind was made up. That one touch of the Holy Spirit gave me the courage to continue the fight for my husband and our marriage.

I knew I must fight for my family. If I wanted a Christian home full of love and peace, I was going to have to fight the enemy and be at peace with myself and my husband. Blessed are the peacemakers!

Many times, I opened the Word and it fed me. More and more I realized that we are in a war for our very soul as well as for our families, friends, and loved ones. We must be a faithful soldier, and never give up the fight. Hope in God's great faithfulness will put a fire in our soul.

Only God can send conviction through the Holy Spirit and break down a stony heart so that person wants to pray. For Ebb, God did just that.

Through all of his illness, he had been on prescribed pain medicine. He wasn't taking them the way they had been prescribed. He was abusing them. He had turned hateful and he had alternating personalities like Dr. Jekyl and Mr. Hyde. He could change in a moment of time.

When our family/church homecoming came around, our grandchildren were there and one of them had accepted Christ as Savior and was on fire for God. He could get by with saying things to his grandpa that nobody else could.

Ebb was sitting at the back of the church when the altar call was made, and the boys asked him to pray. He went forward.

Later he said, "I just couldn't turn them down when I saw the look on their faces."

One day he was outside working and waiting for the scheduled time to take one of his pain pills. He was trying to take them on time and do the right thing with them. He was sort of quarrelsome because of having to wait for the timing of the next pill.

He said the voice of God spoke to him and said, "You don't need them."

He spoke back to God and said, "Well, Lord, if I don't need them, you are going to have to help me!"

When his prescription came, he put it away. He promised God that he would not take another one unless he was in terrible pain and couldn't take it. God blessed him and helped him, but as sure as a person says they are going to do or not do something, temptation will come to test them.

Our youngest grandson had answered the call to preach. He was still very young and didn't have a driver's license. God spoke to Ebb and told him that if he would take our grandson to the places he was being sent to preach, God would give him a long life. So, Ebb was doing that as best he could.

Ebb had been taking Remicade treatments every eight weeks for seventeen years. With the treatments and God's help, he was doing well.

We had an opportunity to go with our grandson where he was scheduled to hold a revival in Alabama. While we were there, Ebb went out with him to look at some old home places and was having trouble with his left hip. We already figured he was headed for a hip replacement when we got home because he had already been in a great deal of pain.

On top of that, he had a tick bite that was inflamed and turned out to be lime disease. He had developed a hacking cough as well.

He was set up for a hip replacement, and planned on taking no pain meds before, during, or after. He also had to have two biopsies of his lungs. He took no pain medicine for any of the health issues during this time.

He had to be taken off the Remicade treatments that he'd had been having for years and couldn't take that treatment any more. My greatest fear was that his Crohn's Disease would come back.

I had lived with him through that ordeal and I knew how horrible it could be, and that it would prevent him from being able to go anywhere. He wouldn't be able to go to church, make any trips with our grandson while he was holding revival meetings, go visiting, or go anywhere.

His future was looking pretty bad.

We made a doctor's appointment and he talked to three different doctors. They told us that he was between a rock and a hard place. All the medicine that worked or helped one thing, would be bad on the other. They told him he was in trouble.

When we came home, we were both very upset by what we'd been told. About all he had to hold on to was what God had spoken to him. I clung to those promises, too.

So many doubts flooded my mind! I needed something personal to help me be strong in my faith. I write prophetic words and promises down. During this season, I read them over and over again. Sometimes when I prayed, I held these written promises up to Heaven and said, *"These words were spoken by my Lord, and they never fail. I choose to believe these words!"*

One day when I was praying for him, I thought about what the doctors had said. In my mind, I saw a beautiful rock walkway. Someone had put a lot of work in on it, but every now and then, I could see a stubborn little yellow head of a dandelion smiling right at me! To me, it looked beautiful.

It made me smile because it looked like hope was alive where there was none. There was hope sprouting up where it looked impossible for anything to grow.

In my heart, there were little flowers of hope.

One night we all went to church except Ebb, who was a prisoner of the bathroom. He was not feeling well at all.

During the service we had gathered around the altar. A young brother in the faith hadn't been a Christian long, but he was full of love and faith. He said he had been praying and when he raised his head, he saw one of our grandson's shoes. He said it came to his mind that the boys and I really needed Ebb to be with us in church.

He was praying in his heart and asking God what it would take for Ebb to have a touch from God and be healed. He said that God spoke to him and told him to fast and pray for three days, without eating or drinking anything. He didn't tell us at the time, so we knew nothing about this during the three days.

On the third day about 10:30 p.m. he called and said he wanted to come and pray for Ebb. He had been very sick that day and we were already ready for bed with our night clothes on. We changed back into our day clothes and waited for him to come.

When this young man entered our house, there was a sense of peace that fell on us. There was a supernatural calmness.

He said, "It is over now, so I can tell you what God spoke to me in your behalf." His lips were parched. It was clear that he was thirsty but had been obedient to what God had spoken to his heart to do. "I've come to pray."

There was no lightning or thunder. There was no mighty wind or great noise. What we felt was the sweet presence of the Holy Spirit.

My husband was immediately healed. He was completely healed right then and there.

We gave this young man a cold glass of water. He drank until his thirst was quenched.

I thought of the verse, *"For whoever gives you a cup of water to drink in My name, because you belong to Christ, assuredly, I say to you, he will by no means lose his reward."* - Mark 9:41

I am so thankful for this young man's love and obedience to God in our behalf. I am also thankful that my husband had put aside the prescription pain medicine that was overtaking his life and changing his personality when God spoke to him about it. Both were obedient, and we experienced the reward.

In my mind, I pondered these questions, *"What if the brother in Christ had not obeyed God? What if he had not had enough love to care for the needs of others? What if he had not fasted and prayed for three days as God had told him to do? What if Ebb had not received his healing and continued to get worse?"*

He has been back to Alabama and anywhere else he wants to go without being plagued by the Chron's Disease. He gives God all the glory

Ebb had a colonoscopy a few days ago. The findings revealed some scar tissue, and a little diverticulitis. There was no sign of Chron's Disease! We give God all the glory for this miraculous healing.

When we are walking through hard times and faced with life's challenges, it can seem overwhelming. Sometimes it's hard to see how God is working behind the scenes or to see the big picture. On the other side of our problems and heartache, we can put the pieces together and see God's love through all of it.

One of my favorite verses is: Now unto him that is able to do exceedingly, abundantly above all that we ask or think, according to the power that worketh in us. (Ephesians 3:20)

Barb Saylor

Great peace have those who love Your law, and nothing causes them to stumble. (Psalm 119:165)

Unanswered Prayers

Samantha Martin

"Lord, you see my heart. There is nothing hidden from you. You know how much I love Greg. You promised that if we ask, you'd hear us and answer."

Have you ever wanted anyone or anything so badly that you stormed the gates of heaven relentlessly, trying to convince God that He should give it to you? Have you ever convinced yourself that God needed to hear from you on the subject one more time and that one more time would release the answer you wanted or make God realize how important it was to you or how He should answer?

There are times when even with our best intent, we misunderstand scripture, or we twist it to fit our own circumstances and cherry pick the verses that seem to fit our situation. This kind of verse picking without reading the whole story in context lacks wisdom. Ministers do it at times to give a reference and bolster the point of their message. People do it because they've been told to take the Word of God and apply it to their lives, so they pick verses that fit what they want in the moment.

I was trying to apply the following verses to my own life in a situation that didn't really fit.

Then He spoke a parable to them, that men always ought to pray and not lose heart, [2] saying: "There was in a certain city a judge who did not fear God nor regard man. [3] Now there was a widow in that city; and she came to him, saying, 'Get justice for me from my adversary.' [4] And he would not for a while; but afterward he said within himself, 'Though I do not fear God nor regard man, [5] yet because this widow troubles me I will avenge her, lest by her continual coming she weary me.' "

[6] Then the Lord said, "Hear what the unjust judge said. [7] And shall God not avenge His own elect who cry out day and night to Him, though He bears long with them? [8] I tell you that He will avenge them speedily. Nevertheless, when the

Son of Man comes, will He really find faith on the earth? (Luke 18:1-8)

This parable about the persistent widow has a whole different meaning than the way I was applying it to my desire for a certain man to fall in love with me. She was persistent. I was persistent. The judge got sick of her knocking on his door, so he answered her to get rid of her. I thought if I prayed long enough and hard enough, God would hear me and answer what I requested because I had asked the same thing so many times. I've heard this passage quoted totally out of context by different ministers to prove a point about persistence.

The widow was seeking justice. She had a righteous and just cause. When the judge responded, he was carrying out his role as a judge (which he should have done in the first place) to provide justice in her case. My cause wasn't just. It was totally selfish. It was me wanting a certain man in my life who I thought would be the answer to all my emotional, physical, and financial needs. Greg could not live up to that fantasy. No one could except Christ working in my life.

God knew I didn't need a man to "fix me." I needed to let God fix me. I needed to redirect my desire to be married, my loneliness, and my dreams about finding the perfect husband into God's care.

At the same time, I was pounding on the doors of heaven to grant my relentless petitions, I also thought I was standing on the promise of God's word in Proverbs 3:5-6 another way. "Trust in the LORD with all your heart and do not lean on your own understanding. In all your ways acknowledge Him, And He will direct your paths."

I wasn't really trusting that God was going to do what was best for me. I absolutely was trusting in my own understanding, which was very limited at the time. I wanted the path that I wanted and didn't want God to direct me away from my heart's cry.

One day while pounding on heaven's gates once again about Greg, the Holy Spirit intervened. I reminded God how much I loved him and all the good I saw in him, convinced that I could bring out his full potential if only he were mine. The Holy Spirit spoke to my mind in a very strong and loving rebuke. *"If you don't stop asking, I'm going to answer your prayer."*

The reality of that one sentence spoken to me by the Holy Spirit shot through me like a lightning bolt! It surely didn't sound like it was a good thing for me to get what I thought I wanted. In that instant, I knew I had been seeking my own will more than God's will for me. Out of God's great love for me, He had not answered the way I wanted. I had been rebuked.

I wept. Then I repented – truly repented.

I had the distinct revelation that if God did answer those hundreds of prayers I'd prayed, asking for Greg, it was not going to be a good thing. The outcome of having him in my life would not be at all what I thought it would be.

I had a whole new understanding of the Lord's prayer in which Jesus instructed us how to pray. "Thy kingdom come, thy will be done (for me and in my life) on earth as it is in Heaven..."

If God was withholding something or someone from my life, it was because of His great love for me and because He had a plan and a purpose for my life in a totally different direction. I could place my future in His hands.

God's plan for me is good. He's directed my paths differently than I anticipated, and in ways I could not have imagined in the time since I prayed all those prayers. I'm still single, but so thankful I did not throw my God given destiny away because of wanting a specific man.

(For I know the thoughts that I think toward you, says the LORD, thoughts of peace and not of evil, to give you a future and a hope. (Jeremiah 29:11NKJV)

Children of the King
Carol Burgess Johnson

The last time I had seen Sheila was on a worship platform where I had been escorted by my ministerial husband, who, along with Sheila's, was helping to lead a Bible camp for teens.

It was the evening after I had spent most of a night in a heap on the living room floor, teetering on the edge of reality. I had waited until my husband was out of town before I searched his office to investigate my growing suspicions. I found what I expected and more. They say a wife is the last to know, but I say the wife overlooks a boatload of inane behavior because she does not want to know. That night I sat with a hammer in my hands, wanting desperately to smash the beautiful anniversary clock Mark had recently given me. He had a jeweler inscribe it with a message of his enduring love, but I had just learned that the brass plate attached carefully to its top hid the message of the original giver's presentation to him.

I could not destroy the clock without waking my two children in their bedroom down the hall. I could not even let loose the wailing that desperately tried to escape my throat, some primal noise growing inside my head. I slid the hammer beneath the sofa as far back as I could push it and heaved in silent pain.

Should I call someone? Who?

Mark's parents were charter members of the church up the hill from this place where I lay. His adult brothers and sisters and their families were a part of the church that had called him to be pastor. If I opened Pandora's box and let this monstrous secret out, it would never go back in. I did not know if I could deal with unleashing such darkness upon my children, upon my extended family, upon the church, and upon me.

I called no one. The next day, however, when Mark called my office and learned I had called in sick, he called me, and I revealed to him what I had discovered. He drove all the way back from camp to convince me that what I knew was true, was not true. I succumbed to the lies as he feverishly pleaded his innocence. He was a victim of, not a participant in, another's fantasies, he told me.

He begged, "Please, please believe me!"

I accepted; no, I grasped at his avowals of innocence. I even returned to camp with him that evening. Would I sing for the campers, he wanted to know? Would I participate in his ministry? I did not realize he had spent the prior week belaboring our unhappy marriage to his colleagues. I did not know he had depicted me as a woman unstable and unsupportive in his commitment to ministry. My return to camp with him was a sign of victory for him before his friends, a sign that God was working in my heart!

So, on that evening, Sheila, who was camp pianist, scooted from the bench as I scooted onto it. I sang my song before the Lord, before hundreds of young people and our ministerial husbands. Sheila played and sang her heart to the Lord that night, also, as she does so beautifully and worshipfully, neither of us knowing what lay before us.

I sang about a Potter who found a broken vessel that no one valued. I sang about how the Potter took all the broken pieces and made a new vessel. I cried out through the song for

God to take this mortal clay and make me over and revive my soul.

The words were prophetic. My brokenness had not yet been completed, but would come with the divorce that lay ahead.

Now, more than thirty years later, the Lord had brought Sheila and me together again in a church, in a women's meeting. "How do I know you?" she asked. She recognized me when I told her who my husband had been.

In the months that followed, Sheila received an invitation from the pastor of Deliverance Church in Kakamega, Kenya to lead a women's retreat. Sheila accepted, and she invited me to be one of ten women on the team. "We can share with these women what God has done in our lives!" We could share with our Kenyan counterparts that God is especially drawn to the hearts of his abandoned daughters, of widows, of the motherless, of those who have been rejected by those they loved and looked to for love. He is the healer of those who were promised bread but received serpents.

Although I did not know how I would go to Kenya, I started praying with the intent that I would go forward unless God closed the door. Sheila met with me and seven other women regularly as we prayed and planned our journey. The tenth "Safari Sister", Gail, would be our preacher for the week; she lived in West Virginia.

I had two barriers to overcome. I could not afford the trip and my health was not good. I was working full-time, and after completing a day's work, my energy was spent. I wasn't sure I had the physical stamina to go, and I certainly did not have the money to pay for the trip. God provided both of these needs in the days and weeks leading up to the journey.

One of our church elders prayed for me after church one Sunday morning that "I would be surprised by wellness." I was! Not only was I in good health during the entire trip, but in all the years since I have not been plagued by the same symptoms. The funds that I needed flowed in from family and friends as they learned about this opportunity.

While we were preparing to go to Kenya, our hearts were stirred for orphans. Sheila began actively seeking a children's home we could visit and take gifts. She located a home in the town of Kisumu and made arrangements for a visit.

The week before we were to travel to Kenya, Sheila contacted us. "You won't believe this, but there is a children's home in Kakamega, and Vicki, the head of this home, is visiting a friend in the U.S. - right here in town!" The friend lived and owned a sewing shop about a mile from the church where most of us worshiped.

We met with Vicki. She shared with us how she had once been an orphan and had endured unending abuse of every kind until one day she felt compelled to take her life. While she was waiting for darkness to fall so she could throw herself into the river, she wandered into a church meeting. That day, instead of taking her life, she came to know Christ, who gave meaning and purpose to her life.

After Christ put hope into her heart, Vicki began taking parent-less children off the streets, one by one. As she spoke with us, each of us Safari Sisters were immediately drawn to Vicki and to the 52 children in her care, and we began planning a visit to her home during our upcoming trip.

Vicki answered our many questions. Vicki personally knew the pastor of Deliverance Church and could assure us he was a devout man of God, highly regarded throughout Kenya.

During those special pre-Kenya moments, we spent with Vicki, the Holy Spirit confirmed in our hearts that the journey before us was ordained by God. We had stepped out on faith, and God indeed had gone before us and prepared the way.

On the day of our arrival, women from Deliverance church of Kakamega travelled many miles to the airport in Kisumu to meet us. They came in a large, un-air-conditioned van over pot-hole filled, red-clay roads. They told us they had come to meet ten American princesses, expecting us to be ten perfect white women living problem-free lives with access to anything our hearts desired! That is what they had observed from their televisions!

We middle-aged American women had been in route more than 20 hours. We met them in our crumpled t-shirts, jeans, messy hair and no make-up, and certainly we were not wearing our weariness well. As we stepped off the plane, the beautiful Kenyan ladies stood waving at us from the airport gate. They were dressed in Sunday's finest, fresh as black-eyed-Susans, undaunted by the meridian heat.

Most days of the Conference we held Bible School classes for the children, and Vicki brought her children when she could. Gail preached powerful messages of hope, and we American women, one by one, shared our stories. We shared stories of brokenness, but through Christ—how our lives had become vessels of power, of love, of sound minds. We shared Christ's deep and unwavering love for us, and how he is especially tender to women who have suffered many things. Sheila shared her story, and I shared mine.

Sometime during the week, Kenyan ladies began confiding to some of us their secrets. Some had suffered abuse at the hands of others, often their own husbands, who, when a marriage is not working, by Kenyan law can take possession of the children and all marital property. Single-again women become outcasts of society, whose women then consider them a risk to their own marriages. A woman's birth family most likely will encourage her to remain with an abusive spouse, knowing that what lies outside the marriage may be even worse than the abuse within it. Many Kenyan women have experienced rejection at its deepest levels.

By the end of the week, some of the Kenyan women, who are stoic by culture (because, after all, isn't life difficult for everyone?) started sharing their stories with one another. When women share their deepest pain and reveal their hidden wounds to each other, that pain can be laid at the feet of Jesus, where there is healing. Two groups of women came together that week. When we, all of us, became honest with each other, we found love and support. We are so very much alike, we daughters of the King.

The Kenyan women discovered ten American princesses (although they were not as they expected), and the ten American princesses discovered a church and town full of Kenyan princesses. Together we discovered unity and rejoicing in the presence of our father, the King, who turned our mourning into dancing!

That initial evening with Vicki in the sewing shop has turned into an ongoing relationship with Victorious Children's Home, a ministry that continues to reach out to homeless children, pulling them from the streets and poverty, providing them with as much home, family, love, ministry, food, and education as Vicki can give. Vicki now is mama to over 150 children in a facility built to accommodate fewer than 50.

Vicki knows the only way out of poverty for her children is through education, and she makes school a priority. Because education is not funded by the government, she must find tuition for each of her children from grade school through college. Several of the older students have committed to helping the younger ones through college once they begin working. There have been times when the children living in the home have agreed to receive only two meals per day so that tuition costs could be met.

I love the heart of Victorious Children's Home! I was able to see Vicki's children enjoy ice cream for the very first time I was privileged to worship alongside them as the children led evening devotions. I experienced their joyful dance and praise, knowing that each had come through much pain and loss during their young lives. Many of her children have lost parents to the HIV/AIDS epidemic that has swept their nation.

Vicki is a woman of both compassion and faith. Sometimes those of us looking in from the outside think, "Why does she take on so much?" Yet, it is evident that God is in the work in this ministry, and He continues to bless and to provide. Although the needs of Victorious Children's Home are great, God provides through the generosity of His people.

"Pure and undefiled religion before God and the Father is this: to visit orphans and widows in their trouble, and to keep oneself unspotted from the world." - James 1:27 (NKJV)

Carol Burgess Johnson

Hope from Hopelessness
(A Continuation from the Previous Story)
Victoria Odundo

On December 31, 1971 child number seven was born to Mr. Aggrey and Sophia M. Odundo. Both were from a small village of Lurambi in Kakamega, Kenya. It was with great joy that they greeted the new child. Perhaps it was not the same level of joy as it could have been for the first child, but it was joy anyway to have a new member in the family of nine. The new baby was given a name, Victoria, which would denote so much meaning in the years to come.

In time, there were two more births. Being the seventh born in a family of nine children did not give me privileges that the kids in small families have. I am talking about scarcity of almost everything, including food.

The experience of a large family teaches a child how to scramble for survival, how to protect his or her self from attack and how to get along in unity to save one's self from hatred and danger. It is important to learn how to live in these big families or you might end up like Joseph; Jacob's son-the dreamer.

My life started on this kind of platform with many siblings ahead of me and a couple behind me. I was sandwiched in the middle. The disadvantage of being among the younger kids in a big family is that if we were having a chicken meal (which came up only at Christmas time), the best part you get is either the chicken's head or feet. If you advance, you get the neck. My part was always the head and my sister Betty's part was the feet.

My parents were very poor, and life was a struggle to raise nine kids on what I would say was almost nothing. So, we were taught life skills; how to work doing the farmhouse chores like washing dishes, washing clothes for the whole family, cooking, fetching firewood from the rain forest, etc. We all grew up learning how to take on responsibilities.

At age four, my dad succumbed to heart problems and my mom was left to raise nine kids as a single parent. This was the genesis of more hardships in our lives. Our uncles took the few things my mom had and chased her out of our little grass thatched house with nine children. Life was never the same again.

My mom went back to her parents' home which was very violent for her and us as her children. In her youth, she had eloped with a Christian man and her strict Islam family had termed her an "outcast" and dead in their lives since she was an infidel.

You may have heard horror stories about concentration camps. Living under my uncles' rule over us was much the same. They were heartless and treated my older siblings like slaves. My mom had to leave after a while with all nine kids. She rented a shanty in the slum area where there were no bathrooms, so every business was done in a dug hole and covered. She still had to pay rent.

My mom had no education because she eloped with my dad at age fifteen. She had been given for marriage by her parents to an older Muslim man as a third wife, so she eloped. Without an education after my father's death, the best she could do was to work on people's farms as a laborer. This became our lifestyle.

A severe drought struck my country in my fifth year of life. The famine was so great that many people and animals died due to starvation and thirst. We hunted for grasshoppers and termites as the only meat we could afford at that time. My mom got wild vegetables from the rain forest which she could not eat herself but cooked for us so that her children had something to eat. She was willing to make this sacrifice for her children

Our country got relief food (yellow flour) but you could not get more than one portion after standing in the line for eight hours or longer. This was not enough to feed all of us.

This kind of hunger makes even the rich cry. Even if you had money there would be no food for you to buy. Stripping locusts came and ate anything green, including grass. Human and animal conflict increased. Both fought for the scarce natural resources.

It was during this time that my life took a sharp turn. My mother could no longer care for nine kids, nor feed us with the food shortages. We were critically malnourished and our need for food was great. My mom gave up all her children to relatives and friends who could afford at least porridge to feed us. In return we were to render them services.

Three of my older siblings committed suicide within a two-year time period. My nephews and nieces started dying at a rate of about one a month. Every other month we lost someone in the family and my mom went into a deep depression. The good Christian woman in her (that she really expressed to the point of being an outcast of the family) disappeared. She started drinking moonshine.

It was in this period of time when there was such need of food that I met my worst nightmare. I lived with many different families.

Due to my quiet nature at the time, I was raped by our neighbor whom I lived with as a house help at age six. He threatened to kill my mother and siblings if I said anything. I had to suffer in silence and keep my wounds inside.

My mom took me to the general hospital after she was told that I was very sick. At the hospital, it was discovered that I had been raped at this young age. I stayed in the hospital for a month to recover, then came back home.

My mother had started living with a man. He was very mean and so were his brothers. His youngest brother hit my sister Betty with an iron rod which busted her forehead. She was airlifted to Nairobi where she lived for a year with doctors.

This man's other brother, who was a sorcerer, raped me at age twelve. He teased me with threats of releasing demons to torment me if I ever told my mom about it.

As I grew older I was distraught and wanted to end my life just like my three siblings had done. I knew it was the only option in life to end my pain, shame, and reproach. Death seemed like a real answer to end my torment. At sixteen, this desire became so strong I decided to go through with suicide. I had everything planned, how to do it, when to do it, and where to do it.

My plan was not one that other people might have chosen, but I gave it a lot of thought and wanted to make sure I would be successful. I was going to have a very quick exit.

I planned to go down to the river in the dark, drown myself and have the crocodiles eat me up. I did not want to be rescued. I did not want any man to ever touch me in an abusive way again. I didn't want there to be an inch of my body left to be abused, even in death. So, I planned to wait until dark when no one would see. No one would come to rescue me from crocodiles in the dark.

On this big day, darkness took too long to come. So, I went in the park to kill time waiting for darkness to fall, determined that I would not have to suffer through another day.

There was a crusade going on there. It was the last thing I wanted to bump into. It was one of those days when you just want to be alone and people keep on bumping into you and wanting to talk. You feel like you might burst with pressure. I didn't want to see nor to talk to anyone.

Boom! There was this crusade going on with over 2,000 people. Of course, there were many who knew me and wanted to talk when they saw me there. Crusade business continued around me and I got myself into this mix. There was no way out because there was no alternative place to hang out.

Stuck in the meeting that I didn't even want to be in, in the first place, you can imagine how I was feeling inside. I was very angry. I was thinking, "GOD, You have been very unfair to me, and now you can't even let me rest in peace! Why must You get into my way?"

Whilst still deep in these angry thoughts, a voice burst from the speaker like a thunder. "I know you are there, exhausted and tired. You have hit a dead end and you want to fall down the cliff. Come up here! I have good news for you!"

The words hit me, and I exclaimed, "That's none of your business, preacher!"

He kept on calling, and I kept on resisting every word that came out of that preacher's mouth! Being overwhelmed with only GOD knew what, I started walking towards the podium! I am telling you that GOD is a GOD who orders our steps. Once I started the journey to that podium, there was no detour! There was an usher along the aisle after every five steps to ensure that there was no escape route in case I wanted to change my mind and didn't want to go to the podium after all.

With ushers escorting me towards the front, I reached my destination, and everyone was clapping their hands, others shedding tears of joy, while others were just praising the LORD.

This preacher introduced me to a Man who turned my life around, forgave my sins and transgressions, changed my name and opened a new chapter in my life. I had a clean page to write on whatever I wanted. This Man to whom the preacher introduced me gave me a second chance for life, and an opportunity to serve HIM. HIS name is JESUS!

My plan was to end my life that day. I thought no one knew what I had in mind. No one could stop me. But God knew, and He had other plans for my life.

7 Where can I go from Your Spirit?
Or where can I flee from Your presence?
⁸ If I ascend into heaven, You are there;
If I make my bed in hell, behold, You are there.
⁹ If I take the wings of the morning,
And dwell in the uttermost parts of the sea,
¹⁰ Even there Your hand shall lead me,
And Your right hand shall hold me.
¹¹ If I say, "Surely the darkness shall fall on me,"
Even the night shall be light about me;
¹² Indeed, the darkness shall not hide from You,
But the night shines as the day;
The darkness and the light are both alike to
You. (Psalm 139:7-12)

When GOD is not done with you, you are not done yet.

GOD turned my pain into a strength that is touching lives even today. Because I know from personal experience what comes from physical abuse and physical hunger, and the abuses that come to children who cannot care for themselves, God has called me to work with children who are just like I was.

I am a mommy to 142 kids residing in *Victorious Children's Home* and mother to over a hundred kids living on the streets that we reach out to with a hot meal and God's love every other Saturday as part of the great commission.

Our vision is to reach out to the hurting world of children with Christlike compassion.

Our mission is to feed one mouth at a time, heal one wound at a time, educate one mind at a time and win one soul FOR CHRIST at a time.

Our objectives are to teach our children life skills to help them be responsible, reliable and respectable people in the society. We give them an education to go into the market place with confidence and compete with others.

We raise our children in Godly principles, teaching them how to love GOD, love people, and have hearts of servanthood.

In conclusion, I want to encourage anyone reading this story that GOD is very faithful. When you are on the edge of the cliff, just trust HIM and hang on! If He can take a life such as mine was and turn it around and give hope to keep on living and a purpose to live for, He can use anyone that will give their heart to Him and let Him do His work in their life.

Pain is inevitable, but misery is a choice. You can change your pain into a strength that can impact lives or into a misery that can make everyone around you miserable.

Forgiveness is the key to the next step, forgive those who hurt you the most as in Matthew 5:43-45.

"You have heard that it was said, 'You shall love your neighbor and hate your enemy.' [44] But I say to you, love your enemies, bless those who curse you, do good to those who hate you, and pray for those who spitefully use you and persecute you, [45] that you may be sons of your Father in heaven; for He makes His sun rise on the evil and on the good, and sends rain on the just and on the unjust."

Forgiveness is not for the other person but for you, even if you are not at fault. May GOD bless you all as you tap into HIS grace.

* * *

Vicki Odundo

Victorious Children's Home

Handidi – Kakamega, Kenya,

Established by Vicki Odundo

(Vicki did not ask me to include this information about the children's home, but her story has touched my heart deeply. I want to share with you the work God has accomplished through one ordinary woman in Kenya who was ready to throw her life away, until God gave her a purpose and a dream. – Judith Victoria Hensley)

The children's home was established in the year 2000 with the purpose of helping children who had lost parents through the HIV epidemic and AIDS in 1990s scourge of this disease. It has become home for many children. Currently almost 150 children live there. Approximately 50 of the children are boys and the rest are girls. Most of the children are school aged in primary, secondary, and tertiary school. They have had some successful students complete their education.

Not only are the children educated but are also given tasks and responsibilities that will help them grow up and become successful individuals as adults. The home is a Christian faith-based one which provides instruction and encourages worship participation.

Victorious Children's Home is Self-Sustainable with the children taking part in animal husbandry, farming, cooking, laundry, and the many tasks necessary to keep the program going.

Needs are many for this children's home. Dormitory living is overcrowded and there is very little space in the facility for storage of resources. Providing and maintaining basic necessities is a constant challenge.

By faith, the children's home has begun work on building an additional structure that will facilitate a dining area and a space designated for church services, a kitchen, and a caretaker's office. Larger dormitories are also needed for both boys and girls.

In Victoria's own words, "God's work is never ending."

- Food and daily needs are $25,000 per year.
- Farming is $2,500 per year.
- Medical Needs; $4,000 per year. Administration $2,000 per year.
- Staff appreciation $10,000 per year

(This information was based on their needs when they housed 62 children. They now have more than 150 children.)

Vicki knows that education is the key to helping children escape poverty, but education is not free in Kenya.

Annual educational needs are:
- College students: $4,750 each per year
- High school students $1,000 each per year
- Elementary students $2,625 per year

New Construction and Land

With Kenya's new constitution, children in orphanages are now required to live in dormitories under the care of a matron. All other staff must live in separate quarters. This will require construction of an additional staff house in the near future.

Land is costly. But, if it can be farmed, it provides necessary space for raising more food and livestock for consumption and sustainability.

To view a video about the work and needs of the children's home, please research this work on Youtube and the internet.

If the Holy Spirit nudges you to be of help to Vicki and the children of Victorious Children's Home, please pray for them, and make a connection or contribution as God leads you.

Below is the correct address for mailing contributions to Vicki through her support team in the USA. ALL donations go completely to the work and needs of the children's home.

Victorious Children's Home
P.O. Box 7435
Kingsport, TN 37664

For you shall go out with joy and be led out with peace; the mountains and the hills shall break forth into singing before you, and all the trees of the field shall clap their hands. (Isaiah 55:12)

In His Time

Karen Hall Gross

"My thoughts are not your thoughts neither are your ways my ways says the Lord." Isaiah 55:8)

Sometimes when we pray about a certain thing we forget or do not think about these words. I began praying for a mate and for God's direction in my life as a young woman while in Bible school.

Right before graduation the director of Southern Highland Evangel, a mission group out of Virginia, came to present opportunities to the students. He was looking for workers to help with youth camp, Bible clubs, and public-school ministry. All I knew at this time was that I had a desire to work with children.

After graduation in 1974 I made plans to work at the youth camp with Southern Highland Evangel in Virginia. That summer I did Bible clubs and worked as a counselor.

While at camp an elderly lady, who was a member of the mission, learned of my desire to work with children. She had a public-school ministry in Virginia, and because of her age she needed a helper. She asked me if I was interested. I was delighted! She talked to the board about it. The board approved and appointed me to work with her.

In September I joined her on the mission field in Hurley, Virginia working with kindergarten through eighth grade in the school ministry. I continued in that ministry and lived there for seven years. I was very well contented working with children both at school, and at the local church.

During this time, I also became a member of Southern Highland Evangel. Through the years I kept praying about a mate only if it was part of God's plan for my life. I was thinking maybe He wanted me to stay single. I was willing to give up my dreams of a husband if that was God's direction.

Life is not without interruptions. The lady I worked with in Virginia retired and moved to California. Also, during this time, I developed an illness which leaves a weakness in the muscles.

With my coworker gone, and the physical challenges brought on by my illness, I could not do the ministry alone. Therefore, in 1982 the mission transferred me from Virginia to Wallins Creek, Kentucky. In the new location, my position was to help another member of Southern Highland Evangel with Bible Clubs, and a public-school ministry.

The first year I was not a happy camper. What a battle there was going on in my mind! I thought perhaps I was out of the Lord's will. After all, if God had place me there, shouldn't I have been happy doing His work there?

As the years passed I still missed Virginia, but learned to love Wallins Creek, Kentucky. Even though I was still single, it was a joy working with the children at school, Bible clubs, and the Baptist church. All the while I continued praying about a mate for my life, but there was no one in sight.

At times, there was a great struggle in my thoughts and desires for my future. I wanted to be married. I wanted a home and family. But I only wanted those things if they included a godly man and God's blessings for our lives together. If I had stayed in Virginia, would there have been a special man there for me? Had my choice to relocate stolen that from me?

At church one day in Sunday School a young lady named Kimberly said to me that she knew a nice man who was a widower and she wanted me to meet him. I told her I was not interested in blind dates.

She pressed the issue and invited me to supper at her house. Reluctantly I gave in and accepted, but I prayed, *"Lord, if this is not Your will, please stop her and cause her not to say anything more about the dinner."*

She didn't, and I said, "Thank you Lord!" I felt that was the answer to my prayer. I'd rather have no man in my life than the wrong man.

One year later, in 1985, a gentleman came as a guest speaker at the church. As I listened I thought, *"I could marry a man like that!"* He had caught my attention.

Later in the year he came back to our church's Homecoming service. At the meal afterwards, we sat together and talked. I noticed Kimberly was keeping an eye on us.

When we returned to the auditorium for the second service, he asked if I minded him sitting beside me.

I said, "Not at all!"

After the service ended I gave him the last of my homemade carrot cake. That began our courtship. His name was Ken Gross. He continued coming to the church and I continued to look forward to seeing him there.

During fellowship time we had during each service where people greeted each other, he would shake my hand and keep holding on to it. He'd say, "I'm going to keep you around!"

I wondered if he was talking about marriage. I was beginning to hope that he was, but still wanted God's plan for my life to be accomplished in whatever the future held. I was still willing to remain single if in that state, I could serve God best. I'm glad God had other plans for both of us.

Soon we began dating regularly. I enjoyed the way he treated me. He made me feel like a queen. He always opened doors for me, pulled out my chair when we ate at meals, took my coat when I came in, held it for me to put it on when I left, and all those gentleman-like things.

Kimberly, the young lady in my Sunday School class, said, "You would have been together a year ago, if you had listened to me."

She was his daughter! Unknown to me, she had been playing matchmaker with him also, trying to get him to meet me. He had told her to mind her own business.

Later, Ken showed me a list he had written in a book of the characteristics he desired in a wife, if the Lord should bring a woman to him. The list was what he wanted in a mate.

As he prayed and asked the Lord for "the right woman" to come into his life, he believed I was the answer to his prayer.

In 1986 we were married. He joined the mission and we serve the Lord together. We celebrated our 32nd wedding anniversary this year.

The doubts I had about being out of God's will, and the fear I had of never being married were unfounded. Looking back, I realize the Lord was in the process of answering my prayers all along. Even when I questioned His will, even when I felt alone and wasn't sure God had a wonderful man to share my life, He was leading me in the right path.

During the years after Ken's wife died, he needed a time to grieve and to heal. In time, he began seeking God for a certain kind of woman with whom he could share his faith and his life. Unknown to us before we met, He was preparing both of us for the answer we were seeking.

God does all things well. Both Ken's prayers and mine were answered in His time.

But the meek shall inherit the earth and shall delight themselves in the abundance of peace. (Psalm 37:11)

Mercy and truth have met together; righteousness and peace have kissed each other. (Psalm 85:10 KJV)

The Lost Earrings

Clelie Bourne

There's nothing remarkable about these inexpensive sterling silver earrings pictured below, or is there?

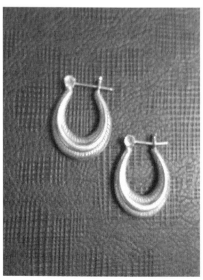

I received them for my birthday more than 30 years ago. Truthfully, I don't remember who gave them to me, but I do remember loving them immediately. I wore them almost all the time, usually for days at a time, taking them out only to shower.

Looking in the mirror one morning, while getting ready for the day, I noticed one was missing. I searched the bed, moving pillows, pulling back sheets and blankets. No earring.

I walked all around the bed looking on the floor, under the bed, between the headboard and mattress, behind the headboard. No earring.

No more time to look for earrings either. I had to go to work.

While driving to work I thought about all the places I had been in the previous 24 to 48 hours and I prayed to God asking Him to help me find my earring.

After arriving at my nanny job, I asked the mom of the little girl I was caring for if perchance she had seen the mate to the remaining earring. I showed it to her, telling her what happened.

Her answer was, "No."

Together we did a cursory search of her kitchen, playroom and the little girl's bedroom. I did not really expect to find it at their house and I didn't. Later that day I searched my car, looking between the seat and back cushions, on the floor boards, under the seats as well as in every crevice I could get my hands into. No earring.

As I said, it's not really an expensive earring, but it's a favorite that I really like and I wanted to find it.

When I got home I did another more thorough, prayerful search of my bedroom and the bed, shaking pillows, pillowcases, sheets and blankets and still no earring. By this time, I was really bummed and had absolutely no idea where that earring could be. It had to be somewhere!

Actually, it could have been anywhere. I was thoroughly convinced the earring was not in my apartment because I had searched it top to bottom. However, it was definitely on my mind and in my prayers, because I really liked these earrings.

Three days later, the alarm went off and I woke feeling something under the pillow. Yes! There, under the pillow, outside of the pillowcase, was my missing earring! Praise God! I don't know where it was for three days, but I know it was not in my bed.

Stay with me because that's not the end of my story. About four or five years ago one of this same pair of earrings went missing again. I don't recall the particulars of how or when I lost it. I just remember when I realized it was missing I prayed, "God you brought it back the last time, help me find it again."

Three days went by, then a week, a month and still no earring. I probably prayed every day for a few months that I would find it. Then I began to think it wasn't all that important.

"It's just an earring," I told myself.

I tossed the remaining one into the turtle dish full of other earrings I wore. Occasionally, when I saw it in there, I'd pray, "God you did it once. Will You do it again, please?"

Eventually, when I noticed the tarnished earring I would only casually wonder what happened to its mate.

Tonight, I was going through my purse that I have carried for almost seven years and have probably emptied and cleaned out at least five or six times over that span.

While attempting to reorganize the contents I emptied a pocket full of electronic gizmos. Deep in the corner I found the missing earring. I hadn't thought about it in a long time. I wasn't even sure I still had its mate. I had given up on ever finding it. Why keep just one earring?

Of course, when I went and looked, there it was in the turtle dish. Once again, I rejoiced. "Thank you, God! You are faithful even when I am not."

The found earring, like it's mate in the turtle dish, was black with tarnish from disuse and neglect. A bit of silver polish and elbow grease made them look brand new.

I don't know why He chose for me to wait this long or why I found the missing earring at this particular time, but I know His timing is perfect.

The earring may have been lost to me, yet God knew where it was. More importantly, when I feel lost and separated from Him, He knows where I am. Even when I can't or don't see or feel His presence, He is with me and knows exactly where I am.

When I come out of hiding, and let His light shine on me once more, I may need a bit of gentle, buffing (sometimes not so gentle), to remove the tarnish that has accumulated from my neglect, just as my earring did. When the buffing is done, I'll be bright as new, the new creation He made of me, ready to be of use to Him, as the earrings are to me.

I am comforted by His promise that I am engraved on the palms of His hands. He will not let me go. He has a plan for me, a future and a hope. He will show me what and where that is, just as He did with the earring, in His perfect timing.

See, I have inscribed you on the palms of My hands; Your walls are continually before Me. (Isaiah 49:16)

Or what woman, having ten silver coins, is she loses one coin does not light a lamp, sweep the house, and search carefully until she finds it? And when she has found it, she calls her friends and neighbors together, saying, 'Rejoice with me, for I have found the piece which I lost!' Likewise, I say to you, there is joy in the presence of the angels of God over one sinner who repents. (Luke 15:8-10 NKJV)

The work of righteousness will be peace, and the effect of righteousness, quietness and assurance forever. (Isaiah 32:17)

When God Directs our Paths

Flo Shell

I don't know anyone who has always been on the correct path in life. I can't say that I began my higher education journey on the right path but assistance from a higher power put me on the right career path.

My studies began in the field of Biology, but I was not successful. I failed a class, was put on probation and denied my student loan. There was a battle going on inside of me. I had my plans made for my future. I studied hard. How could I possibly have failed? I wasn't used to failure. If I was doing what God wanted me to do, how could things go so wrong?

The president of the college came to see me and to bring good news. "You have been misadvised," he informed me. "You are still eligible for your student loan and are not on probation."

I realized then that God had intervened. He was pointing me in a new direction. My major was changed to Elementary Education and as I discovered, that truly was my calling. A series of events made known to me that God had placed me where I belonged. Any doubts I may have had about changing fields of study vanished with the love I had for my position and my students.

How is that for an awesome God? God's plan for our lives is always better than the plans we have made for ourselves!

My teaching career began in a two-room school. I built the fire in a pot-bellied stove, swept the floor each day, and cooked lunch for the students. There were twenty-eight darlings in my room from first grade to fourth. The students were my inspiration to work hard and try to give my best effort for them.

Every day I left school with the feeling, "Job well done! Thank you, Lord!'

My career in education continued to be a blessing. I can honestly say that I loved being a classroom teacher.

There was a massive lay-off of teachers in the county where I worked. Again, I had to struggle with giving up what I loved doing, but feeling that God was leading me in a different direction. After much consideration and deliberation, I decided to retire, and create an opening in my position, so there would be a job available to a younger person.

I was in the public-school system for 33 years. It was not easy letting go of what was familiar and secure. I prayed, and peace overtook my uncertainty about whether or not I was doing the right thing.

God works in mysterious ways. Once my decision was made, and even before I retired, a teaching position was secured for me at Lincoln Memorial University. This was an opportunity to not only assist young people in academics but to grow physically, emotionally, and spiritually. What a great blessing these young adults were to my life!

They were a very positive influence on my well-being. Thank you, God, for my college aged students! I was challenged and rewarded in many new directions as I turned my elementary education experiences gained from all those years in the classroom into teaching educational curriculum at the college level.

I continued my teaching career with great joy and was always thankful that God had guided me to retire from the public-school system at just the right time I would be needed at Lincoln Memorial University.

I had no immediate plans to leave my position on the college level, but eventually it was meant to be. During a summer break I was in Gatlinburg, Tennessee attempting to exit a restaurant and could not get out of the chair. My leg would not move.

After much effort I was able to walk. I was diagnosed with osteoarthritis. Both hip joints needed to be replaced.

I could only manage one procedure at a time. During the right hip joint replacement, the doctor broke my femur bone. Much to my amazement when I found out later, he did not inform me it had been broken at the time of the surgery.

Complications began to occur. I got a staph infection that required a seven day stay in the hospital. This infection lasted about five months. It slowed me down but with the help of God it did not stop me. There were several who thought I should not return to my position at the college, but by strength from a higher power, I went back to teaching after two months.

The students needed me, and I needed them. They assisted me with my every move. They were a great group of young people.

All went well for a while, but then the other hip had to be replaced. I went to a different doctor associated with a different facility. After the ordeal of the first surgery and resulting complications, I was not excited about the prospects of facing it all again. The need for medical intervention became so great, I prayed and trusted that all would be well.

By the grace of God this replacement went great. I was back to teaching in one month. Again, the students assisted me with all my activities.

The next turn in my life happened when my grandson was diagnosed with a brain tumor. Prayer requests were set in motion. He was taken to the Children's Hospital in Cincinnati, Ohio. Prayers were coming from all over the world. Some prayer warriors were as far away as China.

Surgery was performed successfully. Thanks be to God the tumor was not malignant. We had concerns about the impact this surgery might have on his life, but we continued to pray. He is now recognized as a gifted child. This was another answered prayer that came with comfort from above.

One curve after another, one blessing after another, life continued. The next battle we had to face came when my husband became very ill. He required my assistance around the clock. There was another battle to be fought in my mind, although the decision was easy in the end. Should I continue teaching, or was it time to quit?

My love and devotion to my students and for my profession had to be set aside for the love and devotion I had for my husband.

In making my decision to retire from Lincoln Memorial University to care for my husband, I had no idea the length of time that would include, but God knew.

I retired from my college teaching position at Lincoln Memorial University. I had given 49 years of my life to education. The time had come when I was needed at home. Many times, I have given God the glory that I spent the last two years with my husband before God took him to heaven.

After my beloved husband passed, I found myself alone with no partner, no students, and no employment. I became a lonely person and that was something I had never been in my life before. I spent many hours looking at the sky and praying for peace that would pass all understanding.

Time went by slowly, then I began to cope somewhat. There was another calling on my life to answer. My husband's sister needed assistance. She was diagnosed with lung cancer.

I ask God to help her and give me the strength to assist her. We made visits to the doctor for many reasons. Every day that she was able to do so when we went for those appointments, we also went to lunch.

On Sundays we went to church and attended weekly. Going to God's house to worship renewed my strength. The day came when she was no longer meant to be on this earth and God called her home.

Alone again, the Bible was my consolation. Each afternoon I would read the Bible. At the end of three months I had read from Genesis to Revelations with many blessings along the journey. Quiet evenings alone with God provided the strength I needed to survive.

Many ideas and plans crossed my mind. Some of them became a reality and some of them fell by the wayside. I continued to survive through prayer and meditation. Time passed, and I was again alone and lonely. What should I do with my time?

I asked God and the answer came. *"Read, relax, and enjoy each day the Lord has made. There is still a purpose for you that has not yet been fulfilled."*

A group of women at the church prepare meals for the sick, and shut-ins. This became a great mission for me.

One day, I was going to prepare dinner for a neighbor. I had taken a trip to the supermarket to pick up what I needed for the meal I decided to cook. I had a great trip to the grocery store and enjoyed purchasing the items I had selected for the recipe. Having the goal of helping someone in need gave me a feeling of worth and purpose.

Driving home with my groceries, I saw a truck pull across the road directly in my path. I cut the wheel and only hit the back end of his vehicle.

My car went over a curb, down an embankment and stopped upright on a road below the main highway. The door was opened immediately, and I saw two women standing there. One said," This is my friend and she is a nurse."

She pointed to the other lady who then took my hand and helped me get out of the wrecked car. This lady began assisting me. She had a little black bag full of medical equipment. She helped me get seated on the grass and continued talking to me while taking my blood pressure.

She stayed with me until the ambulance arrived and then she was gone. Both ladies were gone. In the flurry of activities with the EMT crew, I didn't see them leave or have time to thank them for staying with me until help arrived.

When I did think about it and asked about them, no one on the scene knew the two ladies, where they came from, or where they went. No one seemed to know who I was talking about.

I ask the policeman if he knew them. He replied, "I never saw anyone that looked like the ladies you are describing."

No one else at the scene may have got a look at them, but I know who they were. My guardian angels were watching over me during my accident. They were there until help arrived and then they were gone.

My car was totaled. However, I was intact. After a complete examination in the emergency room, consisting of eight X-rays and five CAT scans, it was determined my only injuries were bruises from the seat belt.

Again, I could say, "Thank you God!"

This experience was a great eye opener for me. Many individuals have called me lucky. I've gone over the accident and following events in my mind many times. It was not a matter of luck. It was intervention from a higher power.

In reality, guardian angels were there with me. They were not seen in angel form as winged creatures in the way they are portrayed by artists. After this incident, I believe they may appear in any form, age, size or shape.

This most recent chapter in my life has had some ups and downs. A few illnesses have slowed me down but with the help of God, nothing has stopped me. Many things happen in our life to make us stronger in faith, including facing illness. In these difficult times, we draw closer to God.

Retirement is becoming easier to accept and life has become brighter. Missing students is one of my greatest stumbling blocks, but through continuing contact with them I am using it as a stepping stone. Their success is my success.

In this life, every battle and challenge I've faced has been because God was there to help me overcome.

Flo Shell

Therefore, having been justified by faith, we have peace with God through our Lord Jesus Christ. (Romans 5:1)

The Spirit of Fear and The Seductive Voice of Suicide

Rhonda Long Robinson

"For God hath not given us the spirit of fear; but of power, and of love, and of a sound mind."
(2 Timothy 4:10)

"I can't do this God! I can't go through what my mom went through..."

That day nearly twenty years ago still burns in my memory. My beautiful godly mother had passed away from Lou Gehrig's disease. I had cared for her during the three years leading up to her death and had to watch as she suffered from this hideous disease. I saw her wither away to a shell of her former self, with her mind fully intact.

A year after her death, I found myself engulfed with fear that this illness was taking hold of me. I could not bear to think the same disease I had watched take not only my mother, but my grandmother, and uncle as well, was in my own future.

The spirit of fear is identified in 2 Timothy 4:10. *"For God hath not given us the spirit of fear, but of power, and of love, and of a sound mind."* This verse lets us know that fear is a spirit.

I had begun to feel the same symptoms in my feet as those which had started in my mother. I wrestled in silence with my fears. I had been an adventuresome and strong girl and young woman. In my twenty-nine years, I had been through some difficult times, but never contemplated suicide.

I had always had a strong will to live. One particular night, I was home alone. My husband and ten-year-old daughter were gone to a basketball game. In this moment of fear and weakness a seductive voice, that sounded a lot like my own voice, began to offer a solution to my fear and anxiety about my problem.

But how could I do this! I did not want my daughter to grow up knowing her mother had done such a thing. I did not want my family to blame themselves.

The voice in my head began to solve this problem as well. "Make it look like an accident." With sorrow gripping my heart, I began to rehearse this possible scenario in my head.

Later that night I went to bed with this silent battle in my head. In the dark hours of the night I was awakened by a different voice, a voice that was audible. It woke me from my sleep.

This voice spoke clearly and with great love and authority. "Don't entertain the enemy!"

I was fully awake. This voice, the very voice of God, dispelled the voice of death and darkness that was trying to engulf me. With great rejoicing I cried, "I will not die! God means for me to live!" I felt it as a promise that I would not die from this disease.

Therefore, submit to God. Resist the devil and he will flee from you. Draw near to God and He will draw near to you. (James 4:7-8)

The trouble is that we don't always recognize the enemy. Not long ago I heard someone say, "Do you know who Satan looks like? He looks like you and sounds like you."

I was entertaining the enemy. I was not resisting him. The seductive voice of suicide had been weaving itself around me. The trouble was that I thought it was my own voice seeking and finding a logical solution to my desperation.

My heart was full of joy when I recognized the enemy of my soul as the whisperer that had been tormenting my thoughts. The generational curse was broken, and I would live.

The fear was gone, and stayed completely gone for a few short months, until the symptoms manifested again. The spirit of fear came back to attack once again. The familiar feeling of numbness had returned. With every trip and stumble, fear gripped me.

Once again, a voice woke me up from sleep in the middle of the night. This time God said, "Shake the serpent into the fire!"

When I woke up, I was startled. I knew the story in the Bible to which this applied. It was the story of the apostle Paul and what happened to him when he was shipwrecked on an island.

"And when Paul had gathered a bundle of sticks, and laid them on the fire, there came a viper out of the heat, and fastened on his hand.

But when Paul had gathered a bundle of sticks and laid them on the fire, a viper came out because of the heat, and fastened on his hand. [4] So when the natives saw the creature hanging from his hand, they said to one another, "No doubt this man is a murderer, whom, though he has escaped the sea, yet justice does not allow to live."

5 But he shook off the creature into the fire and suffered no harm. **6** However, they were expecting that he would swell up or suddenly fall down dead. But after they had looked for a long time and saw no harm come to him, they changed their minds and said that he was a god." (Acts 28: 3-6 KJV)

What was God trying to tell me? The snake had bitten me. If I kept believing I was going to die, I was going to. The enemy of my soul was striking. He didn't care if I left this earth by disease or suicide. I shook the snake into the fire twenty years ago.

The enemy has tried to strike me many times throughout the years, but every time this fear tries to take hold, even when I feel the symptoms, I SHAKE IT OFF! Jesus gives us a prescription for anxiety (rooted in fear).

Philippians 4:6-7 instructs us, "Do not be anxious about anything, but in everything by prayer and supplication with thanksgiving let your request be made known to God."

I remind myself of this when the spirit of fear tries to strike again.

Fear is a spiritual battle and one that must be fought in the realm of the mind.

Ephesians 6:12-17 says, "For we wrestle not against flesh and blood, but against principalities, against powers, against the rulers of the darkness of this world, against spiritual wickedness in high places.

13 Wherefore take unto you the whole armor of God, that ye may be able to withstand in the evil day, and having done all, to stand.

14 Stand therefore, having your loins girt about with truth, and having on the breastplate of righteousness;

15 And your feet shod with the preparation of the gospel of peace;

16 Above all, taking the shield of faith, wherewith ye shall be able to quench all the fiery darts of the wicked.

17 And take the helmet of salvation, and the sword of the Spirit, which is the word of God:"

God has spoken, and I believed. I knew I could not walk in faith and fear at the same time. I had to bring every thought into captivity and not let it take hold.

Proverbs 18:21 declares, *"Death and life are in the power of the tongue: and they that love it shall eat the fruit thereof."* (KJV)

We have to guard our heart, minds, and what come out of our mouth. We need to speak life to ourselves.

If Paul had believed he would die from the viper's bite, he surely would have. The enemy was not only trying to kill Paul, but the work of God in him. He feared what Paul was going to be! What is the enemy afraid of in us individually?

Under the enticement of the spirit of fear, I could not see the hope for my future. I was blinded by my pain. I could not see the future I would have with my husband, or the adventures we would share. I could not see how much my daughter would need me. I could not see the son who would need a mother. I could not see or hear those that would sweetly call me "Nonna," and could not see the countless students that would pass through my door and bless my life. I could not see myself standing in front of rooms full of youth at risk as a clinical counselor, helping them (through the grace of God), to break their own generational curses.

Twenty years later I am still standing. The generational curses of sickness, depression, and suicidal thoughts are broken. Had I committed suicide I would have started a generational curse for my children and grandchildren to fight.

When I read 2 Corinthians 10:4 I am reminded of the source of our battles and our source of victory. "For the weapons of our warfare are not carnal, but mighty through God to the pulling down of strong holds."

My battle was fought so that not only I could be free to live, but my children and future generations that will come from me will not have to walk under the devastation, shame and grief that come to families of those who have committed suicide. Strongholds have been pulled down in the name of Jesus!

Rhonda Long Robinson

Behold, I will bring health and healing; I will heal them and reveal to them the abundance of peace and truth. (Jeremiah 33:6 NKJV)

Trust in the Lord with all your heart, And lean not on your own understanding; Proverbs 3:5)

Stay or Go?
Judith Victoria Hensley

As a resident in a small rural county in southeastern Kentucky, I loved the mountains and the people. I was involved with the Eastern Kentucky Teacher's Network through the Foxfire National Teacher Training Program and opportunities in the center of the state were many. My son had been accepted to the University of Kentucky as an undergraduate student and was a freshman living on campus in Lexington. I missed him terribly.

Several teachers within the network encouraged me to begin to look for jobs in the central part of the state. My training in the network and successful classroom projects had begun to gain attention. There were many open doors for providing professional development to other teachers and school systems. There was the potential for career advancement and better pay.

When I was approached about interviewing for a job I hadn't even been looking for, I questioned whether it was God's way of swinging a door open in front of me and telling me it was time to change course in my life. The battle began in earnest in my mind. Should I go, or should I stay?

When the call came, the secretary set up an interview date for me to meet with the Superintendent of Schools in a lovely county right outside of Lexington, Kentucky. I had spent five years in the city while my former husband was completing his graduate studies at the University.

I liked the area. It was familiar to me and centrally located in the state. I still had friends and relatives in the area. Perhaps I would have other opportunities to meet new people as a single adult.

I prayed all the way up the interstate during the three-hour drive to the interview. "Father, if YOU have opened this door, give me the courage to walk through it. If this is the direction You are leading me, please let everything go smoothly and let me get the job."

I did not have peace about anything but decided that I was giving in to fear of the unknown and the least I could do was go to the interview.

My parents and many family members and friends would be three hours away. I would have to find a new church, a new place to live, and in many ways felt as if I would be starting from scratch again. I hated the idea of packing up everything and having to move to a new place on one hand, but the possibility was exciting on the other hand. It would be an adventure.

I was convinced that God was in the arrangements. I let myself begin to be excited. My imagination set in.

Much to my dismay, when I arrived, the secretary told me the Superintendent had gone out of town on vacation and would not be there to conduct the interview. When I asked if someone else was available to speak with me since I had made the long drive up, I was curtly dismissed without speaking to anyone else.

The battle in my mind amplified. They had contacted me, and not the other way around. They had set up the appointment and told me when to come. They had reached out to me. I had not been in pursuit of anything. How could they have gotten the dates so wrong? Why hadn't someone contacted me and rescheduled before I made the long drive up?

I started wondering if the devil had gotten in the arrangements and was just trying to block me from a blessing. I was frustrated and confused, disappointed, and a little bit angry. I had been dismissed without so much as speaking to anyone else in administration or being given any information at all.

The further I drove, the more conflicted my thoughts became. I certainly had no peace about any of it. I simply couldn't understand how things had gotten so confused.

Finally, I prayed, "Lord, I'm willing to move if you want me to move. I'm willing to stay if you want me to stay. But where ever I go or stay, I need a house and a place to call my own. I don't want to pay rent forever. I want my son to feel like he has a home to come to."

Suddenly a voice spoke clearly to me, "Go home and call _____ (a specific person) at _____ Bank. Tell them you are looking for a house."

It was as if someone was sitting in the car with me and gave me clear, precise instructions. I knew the person's name but did not know them personally. I had no idea what position they held at the bank. I didn't even know what I was supposed to say to them when I got them on the phone.

However, the experience had been so unusual, I called as soon as I got home. I asked for the lady by name. When she got on the phone, I stumbled around and asked her if she had a house for rent.

No, she did not. But the bank had a house on which they were taking bids. It turned out that she was one of the vice presidents of her bank in charge of loans. I made an appointment to see the house.

It was a large looking house in the city limits that had set empty for a while. Weeds had grown as tall as second floor the windows. When I walked inside, the color scheme and wall paper were about the ugliest thing I had ever seen. The house was in need of repairs AND tender love and care. I saw the potential and not the drawbacks.

I knew the house was already mine. Hadn't God spoken directly to me about it? Had He given me an answer to my prayers about whether or not I should stay in my hometown or move three hours away and in effect start my life anew? God doesn't make mistakes.

There was another party bidding on the house. I prayed and asked God where my cut off point should be, and what could I realistically handle financially. I was very comfortable with the specific number I heard.

The house had a full basement with half as a garage, all the living space on the upstairs floor, and above that a full attic. The bids were low, but it needed a great deal of fixing up.

I asked a lady at the bank what day I could pick up the keys, confident that the house was mine. She told me the bidding had stopped and the other person had the high bid. I had lost out.

Not to be dissuaded, I asked the Lord what was going on? Had I misunderstood? Hadn't I called the person He told me to call at the bank He told me to call? Hadn't I bid the price I felt in my heart the Lord had spoken to me? What in the world had happened?

Again, that strong direct voice spoke to me, "You'll have the keys by Friday."

I called the bank the next day and told them, "When they change their mind, just call me and let me know. I'll be there to sign the papers."

The lady, by this time thinking I was a little off my rocker said, "Honey, you did not get the house. The other couple got it. They won the bid. Their loan has been approved. The house is THEIRS."

Realizing that she didn't know what I knew, I said, "Just give me a call when you want me to come and pick up the keys."

I heard nothing for the next couple of days but went about my business. When I got home on Thursday evening, there was a message on the answering machine from the bank, asking if I was still interested in purchasing the house. It was too late to return the call that day.

I went to the bank Friday morning, all smiles, and said, "I'm here to pick up the keys for my house."

I remember that she didn't ask any questions, didn't say anything, but shook her head in disbelief as she ushered me into the right office of the original lady I'd called. The paperwork was ready.

The keys were mine on Friday. The house was mine as soon as everything was processed.

I moved in during one of the hottest July heat waves on record with no air conditioning. My parents, friends, and acquaintances helped me move my belongings from the house I had been renting to the house that was to be my home for the last twenty years.

I have never wondered about whether I made the right decision to stay. God had made it clear. There may have been other good opportunities for me had I relocated all those years ago, but there have been more than enough here where I stayed.

If I have to make the decision again in my lifetime, I am confident that God will prepare a place for me not only in heaven, but on this earth as well, exactly where He wants me to be.

Judith Victoria Hensley

Finally, brethren, whatever things are true, whatever things are noble, whatever things are just, whatever things are pure, whatever things are lovely, whatever things are of good report, if there is any virtue and if there is anything praiseworthy—meditate on these things. (Philippians 4:8)

Keep your heart with all diligence, for out of it spring the issues of life. (Proverbs 4:23)

The Christmas Tree
Geraldine Middleton

Right after I got out of nursing school, I decided to buy a trailer. The house I was living in had so many leaks, it took about fifteen pots and pans to catch the water that seeped through the roof. When it rained on the outside, it rained on the inside.

My husband wouldn't help me move into the trailer. I was pushing him hard, but he had no intention of helping me.

It was about two or three weeks before Christmas. I was really frustrated with him and with the whole situation. My mind was tormented with the desire to move and not able to move everything by myself.

I was very angry. I wanted something better than the house we were living in. It seemed to me like he didn't care one way or another. There was a real battle going on in my mind.

I gave him an ultimatum. "If I don't get moved into the trailer before Christmas, I am NOT putting up a Christmas tree!"

God had other plans for me. He was more interested in my heart than in me getting out of the house and into the trailer.

One evening I was sitting on the side of the couch that let out into a bed where I slept. I wasn't expecting anything special to happen, but God showed up and gave me a vision.

I saw three flashes of the most beautiful Christmas tree I ever saw in my life. I knew that me refusing to put up a Christmas tree that year was not how I should be thinking or acting.

I told the Lord, "If this is the way You want me to live, it's okay."

So, I put up a Christmas tree in the old leaky house. My heart changed.

It was as if me putting up that Christmas tree was very important to my husband. He changed! He was acting so happy!

He started helping get things ready to move into the trailer. We didn't move until after Christmas, but there was such a peace in that old house! There was peace between us and peace in me.

I knew God was going to change things in my life. Years have passed since that Christmas. God has done many wonderful things in my life and seen me through many challenges.

I give God praise for all He has done for my family.

And do not be conformed to this world, but be transformed by the renewing of your mind, that you may prove what is that good and acceptable and perfect will of God. (Romans 12:2)

For God has not given us a spirit of fear, but of power and of love and of a sound mind. (2 Timothy 1:7)

Overcoming Grief
Shirley Denton

As a young teenager I was caught up in a life of mixed emotions. I was constantly fighting battles in my mind that I couldn't talk about. My Mother decided to move out of the house, and later divorced my father. It was then I decided to move out.

I couldn't take the disappointment and constant arguing. At the age of 18 I married the man with whom I had fallen in love, but when I got pregnant things changed for the worse.

My husband was very abusive mentally. His constant berating caused me to slip into a deep depression.

I continued going to church and asking God to rescue me. Then one day after I was almost killed God showed me a way out and the courage to leave. God became my strength and helper. I have never forgotten His magnificent mercy toward me.

I had three children from that marriage. I had a daughter and two sons which I raised by myself.

The years passed by.

In the year of 1996 my younger son had a brain bleed causing uncontrollable seizures. The brain surgeon estimated that he might have three days to live.

From the hospital I called my church asking for prayer for my son. My mind was torn up. I was desperate. I knew they prayed for my son and also prayed for me.

Each day seemed like it was a week long. Three days passed, and my son was still alive but continued to have horrible seizures. I took him home after one week in the hospital. Although the seizures disabled him, I was so thankful that God spared his life.

I began thanking God for his mercy and love. He held me up and held me together when I felt like I couldn't take another day.

Years passed before I faced another heartbreaking event. My oldest son had a heart condition. He was being treated in the hospital at the University of Kentucky. I received a call saying my son was dying.

The doctor informed me that I could come and care for him or they would put him in hospice. I began to pray to God, telling him there's no way I could help my son through the dying process. He was only given a few days to live.

I cried and talked to the Lord. "Please help me! I can't do this!"

The Lord spoke to me saying, "You can and must do this for your son. I will lead you through this, my daughter."

I moved to Kentucky and rented a house. I picked up my son from the hospital, brought him home, and began caring for him. He lived for another three months. Those three months were such a blessing to him and to me. Not only did we get to spend precious time together, but I also led my son to Christ.

The morning he passed away was in 1999. I held his hand and prayed with him while he was dying. God was so loving and merciful to me on that sad day. He held me in his arms and kept me from falling apart.

I moved back to Ohio shortly after his death.

One month later I found my father dead from a heart attack. He had been dead for three days when I found him. The combined grief for my son and the loss of my father overwhelmed me. I cried out to the Lord constantly. I was drowning in sorrow.

My grief had tripled. Sorrow bound me to a rollercoaster of emotions. I started having anxiety attacks. The Lord knew I would look to Him for comfort and peace of mind and He was always there for me when I needed Him.

The Lord loved me so much that He gently spoke to me. "Daughter, don't you remember that when I died, my own mother grieved at the foot of the cross? She wept for me because I had to die."

More years passed by. I was still healing and working through the grief of losing my loved ones. Each day brought a battle of emotions and a battle with my thoughts and grief.

I found a book written by a lady minister about the battlefield of the mind. What a wonderful book! It spoke to me in a way that I needed and could understand. I drew strength from reading and rereading those pages.

In the year of 2004 my only daughter was losing her battle with juvenile diabetes. The complications of the disease were many. This was another long and tiring journey on top of all the grief I had already been through.

The morning of June 12 when I found her dead, I cried out to the Lord, "No! Not again! Have mercy on me, Lord! I can't go through another death!" I was desperate for help beyond myself.

Jesus spoke loud to me, "Yes, my daughter, I will help you and comfort you."

My daughter had two daughters of her own that were left without their mother. One was 8 years old one was 15. On top of losing her, I had to go through the legal procedures to get custody of them.

My grief was overwhelming. It consumed all joy from my life. I started walking, praying, and crying as I walked. It became a routine. I couldn't find any peace in my mind. My thoughts were tormented with questions I couldn't answer.

Then the Lord spoke to me about how the Word of God is healing to the mind. At first, I didn't understand what He was saying to me. The Lord was patient with me and spoke the same message to my heart three times before I understood.

I started reading the scriptures in the Bible. I let the Word of God speak to me. The power of the Word began to do its work in my mind and heart.

I felt so alone. I was abandoned by my family. They never called or came by to check on me or the girls. It was a very discouraging time in my life.

I put my trust in the Lord and believed He would be there for me. His Word promised that He would never leave me or forsake me.

Daily I walked and talked with Jesus. He was my friend, my Comforter, my Savior. He healed my broken heart and my troubled mind.

My long journey through grief taught me so much about life and death. My spiritual eyes and mind began seeing things all new. I began to look at life differently. I began to realize how wonderful and powerful God's love is for all his children.

I believe that losing a loved one is one of the most powerful sorrows a person must ever go through. Watching a loved one suffer is also heartbreaking. My beloved daughter was 35 when she passed. She had become blind and went through kidney failure. Her suffering was great. My mother's heart suffered with her.

My oldest son was 30 when he passed away. His heart slowly gave out. I will never forget my children. My journey through grief has been a long one.

Looking back, I am amazed at the strength and comfort my Blessed Savior was to me. I give all praise and thanks to Him for carrying me through the darkest times of my life. Without Him I know in my heart I would have drowned in darkness and depression.

Because of the road I've traveled through life, I now share what my grief journey taught me to others who have experienced loss and must pass through the grieving process. I understand the pain of their loss. I understand their unspeakable sorrow. I understand the battles they fight in their mind as they try to make sense of things that were beyond their control.

And I share hope. I have been where they are and by the grace of God I have overcome my troubled mind and found His peace in each situation. One glorious day I shall be reunited with my children and worship our magnificent Savior eternally. We will share a Heavenly paradise in our reunion.

If then you were raised with Christ, seek those things which are above, where Christ is, sitting at the right hand of God. ² Set your mind on things above, not on things on the earth. (Colossians 3:1-2)

Call to Me, and I will answer you, and show you great and mighty things, which you do not know. (Jeremiah 33:3)

Strength and honor are her clothing; and she shall rejoice in time to come. (Proverbs 31:25)

Coping with Grief and Loss
Karen Bruce Gross

When I was a child, we lived in a coal camp at Mary Helen in Harlan County, Kentucky. On March 8, 1965 it was a cold sunny day with the wind blowing as I walked home from school with my friend, Tommy Gross.

Tommy's uncle and aunt, Otis and Louise Gross lived across the creek from us in the coal camp. Otis had a big family of ten children. Most of the children living in Macaroni Hollow would gather up in Otis Gross's yard to play. When we got home from school, some of the boys were going to play ball in Otis's yard.

Brothers Rodney, Ralph, and George Gross were going up on the mountain instead of playing to get coal to heat their house. They were going to an old abandoned mine. With a hatchet and simple tools to dig the coal out of the abandoned spot and little grass sacks to carry the coal back home to be used to heat the house, they went to their chore.

Tommy Gross, Dennis Robinson, and Leon Walker were going with them. My brother David and Allen Robinson were young boys. They started to follow the older boys up the mountain. Dennis and Leon returned to bring the younger boys back and make them stay home.

Suddenly we saw people running up the road. Ambulances, trucks, and cars were also going up the road toward the mine. My mom, brother Danny, sister Janet, and I were at home when we heard people screaming.

We couldn't understand what was going on, but we knew it wasn't good. An explosion or roof fall inside the coal mine was something every wife, mother, daughter, sister, and sweetheart of a coal miner feared.

Mom went out to find David. We stood on the porch watching. Dennis came over and said there was a cave in at the mines where the Gross boys had gone to get coal.

We saw someone bring Ada Gross home from the hospital where she worked. The news was bad. Three ambulances came slowly down the road. Three young boys had been killed by a large rock fall. Rodney was 17, George was 12, and their cousin Tommy was 13. Ralph Gross escaped the cave-in.

A cold drizzle set in and the sky had darkened. An eeriness settled over the community as the ambulances started their journey.

I can still hear Louise's scream in my mind as the ambulances came down the mountain. She was the mother of two of the young boys who had been killed. We were all in shock.

Some days I would walk up to the face of the mine where the tragedy happened and sit there thinking. I was very young, but the battle raged in my mind about life and death and the loss of these three young people that I knew. I couldn't help wondering why these three boys had died this way. It didn't make sense to me.

The three little burlap grass sacks of coal the boys had gathered before the cave-in were left sitting there until they rotted.

Why was I still alive? What was my place and purpose in life? Why did God let them die? What happened to a person when they died? My mind was an ocean full of unanswered questions about life and death.

The tragedy that killed the cousins brought friends and family to Oscar Gross's house. My mom was hired to fix lunch and sit with Oscar's dad while Oscar and Ada worked. That was her financial contribution to our family. Work had to go on, even in the middle of tragedy.

Mom was at their house when she met Bill. She came home and said, "Karen, there is a good-looking boy out at Oscar's."

The day of the funeral, I met Bill, my future husband, for the first time. It was his19th birthday. He was good looking with a big smile. He was friendly and flirty.

I was very shy. I tried to hide it from everyone, but at the age of 13 I was smitten.

When Bill first came to Harlan, he stayed at Oscar Gross's house with his papaw who had raised him. We would see each other from time to time. He occupied a lot of my thoughts.

Bill was six years older than me, but he would tease me. "Do you love me?" he'd ask.

"NO!" I'd answer.

"Well, I love you!" he would say. He always made me laugh.

Bill was drafted into the Army. He asked everyone to write to him. He was stationed in Hawaii at first. Eventually, everyone stopped writing to him except me and some of his friends from Knox County where he grew up.

I was the only one in my family who attended church regularly at that time. I always went and participated in youth programs and whatever was going on at the church. The other young people would be going in their own directions, dating, doing their own thing, but I was always the one going to church.

I prayed for my family and friends. I prayed for Bill and asked God to keep him safe.

Before coming home, he wrote to me and said, "You are my girl, and don't' you forget it!" He also said he was coming home to me. He did.

He came home in January 1968. It was four days before my 16th birthday. He was wild, and I was young. I was all in for whatever was going to come. I loved him, and I was sure I wanted to spend my life with him.

We were married on August 26th, 1968 and I did not start my senior year of high school. At 16 I was a married woman and a married woman's place was at home, keeping house and having babies. It was time for me to grow up and be a good wife to my husband.

In our culture, that was the expected thing. It was the goal of young women at that time. I felt very blessed to be in love, married, and have a place of our own.

Bill went to work for Coal Resources at Mary Helen. He was hired to pick slate out of the coal as it went down the belt line. He was always a good worker, but he had a problem with alcohol and PTSD.

Bill couldn't resist alcohol no matter how hard he tried. Every week-end he would say he quit. While he was out running around with his buddies and drinking, I would go back home to Mom and Dad's until he came to get me.

I always went to church, even when he didn't go with me. I couldn't deal with his drinking on the week-ends and worry about where he was or what he was doing. Going back to my parents' house and going to my home church made me feel safe and secure. I knew he'd always come and get me, wherever I was.

He was having nightmares and night sweats from the PTSD. Some nights he would shake the bed so hard I was afraid to touch him or startle him because he would come up fighting. I didn't know what was going on and I had not expected anything like that to be part of our marriage.

Most of the time I would stand in the doorway and call his name or say, "Honey, are you all right?"

He would wake up and say, "Yes."

Bill had been through so much in his young life. He had lost his three cousins in the cave-in, been through Vietnam and the horrors of war, lost two baby sisters in a house fire, and then lost his mother tragically. I loved him through all of it.

Bill was under conviction about things in his life that needed to change and the state of his soul. I prayed, and things got worse. I prayed and sought every piece of advice that other Christians gave to me about how to pray and how to live with a husband with problems.

On Saturday night before Easter in 1975, my uncle Everette Bruce and his wife, Louise came in from Michigan to visit Mom and Dad. My uncle had been a bad drinker like Bill.

Everette had accepted Jesus as his Lord and Savior a couple of years earlier. We sat and talked about how happy their family was with them serving the Lord together. They had a really good life after he gave his heart to God. As a couple they were so happy and talking about what all God had done for them since Everette God saved. I wanted that for my family. I just wanted a little of what they had.

As they left my mom and dad's house that night, I asked God to give me just a little bit of happiness like theirs. I was pregnant and wanted a Christian home where we would raise our children in church and attend as a family.

Bill had gone to the lake with some of his friends that week-end. They had been partying and fishing, like usual. He came back home on Easter Sunday.

One of Bill's friends, Kenneth Robison, was at the lake with him. He said Bill was very, very sick at the lake. Kenneth said Bill told him, "If I ever get home, I will not be in this shape ever again."

He called me after church on Sunday when I was at mom's and asked me to come home and take him out to see the preacher. I asked, "Are you sure?"

As much as I wanted him to make things right with God, and as many prayers as I had prayed for that very thing, I wanted to know it was a true decision on his part. He said he was sure. So, we went to talk to Craig Lyman, the pastor of my church. Bill accepted Jesus as his personal savior.

Three days later I gave birth to a beautiful baby girl. On the day Misty was born, Bill sat reading his Bible instead of raising a fight with the doctor or one of the medical staff which I was afraid he might do.

Bill's life changed. He completely quit drinking. He still had PTSD with nightmares and night sweats, but it wasn't as bad. All our lives changed for the better.

Bill was always a good worker, but after he gave his heart to God, he really was serious about mining. He studied electricity and got his "bossing" papers. He took every class he could for additional mining card certifications. He became manager of mining for GW New Horizon Coal Company.

In 1981 he started his own trucking company to haul coal for New Horizon. I did all the book work in the business and hauled parts and oil for the trucks. We were both working and raising our family together.

I didn't think anything about whether or not I could do it. It had to be done, so I just did it. I didn't know how to do everything at first, but I learned on my own to do what I had to do. I had to learn how to deal with the men who operated the supply companies that provided truck parts. Some were very arrogant, but I learned to stand up to them. I had to learn how to do the banking, payroll and payroll deductions, and everything that had to do with the trucking business.

When doubts entered my mind, I always asked the Lord to guide me, direct my paths, and help me. He always has.

In 1984 Bill passed out at work. The doctors said Bill had a bad aortic heart valve and must have surgery.

He had open-heart surgery in August and a metal valve was inserted. He was on blood thinner. Because the need for this medication was long term and he would have to take it, Bill qualified for automatic disability, but he refused to retire. He wanted to work. He liked to work.

We knew he would have to retire early, but he remained determined to work for as long as he possibly could. Mining was starting to decline, and we knew if the mine closed, the trucking company would also suffer.

I began to think about other options of what kind of job I could get to help us out, or if maybe I should go back to school and earn a degree that would help me land a better job with better pay.

Neither my sister, Janet, or I had graduated from high school. We talked about getting our GED as an equivalent to the diploma we didn't get for finishing high school.

I cannot remember anyone ever telling me I could go to college. No one encouraged me to think about pursuing my studies or think about a career that required a college degree. I was meant to be a wife and mother and I had done that instead of going any further in school.

One day Janet stopped by the house and said she had signed both of us up to take the GED test. She wanted me to take the test with her. I let her talk me into it. I had always felt dumb because I hadn't finished high school, but I was willing to try. We took the test, and both passed.

My friend, Terri Brock, was taking college classes, working and raising her family. I had another friend, Debbie who was calling me all the time and needing good advice. I didn't feel qualified enough or educated enough to be able to help her the best way possible. She was afraid of cancer.

I felt like I needed to get an education to help Debbie and others who needed answers I didn't know how to give. At first Bill did not like the idea of me going to school, but in time he came around to the idea.

I graduated in 1995, the same year the mine operation closed. In 1996 I went to work at the local Appalachian Regional Hospital as the Social Worker/Discharge Planner. While I worked at the hospital I went on to Lincoln Memorial University in Tazewell, Tennessee to get my Masters' Degree. Bill was very proud of me and I was happy to achieve my goals.

I had always asked God to direct my paths and it was obvious that He had been directing me all along. God's timing in my life was perfect.

Bill stayed home and took care of the house. We swapped places. After our daughter Misty had children, he helped her when she had to go to the doctor. During summers, he kept our grandchildren Will and Aaron most of the time, taking them fishing and camping along with their cousins, Cassidy and Gavin.

Bill started going to the VA at Johnson City, Tennessee for multiple medical problems. In 2011 when Bill went to the VA, the girl doing the Echo gasped, then said she would be back. She hurried out and got the cardiologist.

He came and looked at the screen, and said, "I see it."

Bill had an aneurysm that was 10 cm on his aorta. My brother David had gone to the VA Hospital with Bill that day. The doctor wanted him to stay, but Bill insisted on coming home.

He would not go back that evening, but he went the next day. He said, "I don't want to do this!"

I said, "I will make you!" I wanted more time with him and I knew he had to do this.

I worried and cried all evening. I prayed and asked God to help us. My mind was filled with the fear of spending any part of my life without this man I had loved since I was a child. I fell asleep curled up against him.

When we arrived in Johnson City the next day, the doctor said he didn't think Bill would return. Arrangements for the surgery were made at Duke University. An ambulance was being scheduled to transport him because the air pressure from a helicopter flight could have caused the aneurism to rupture.

As I headed out of the hospital in a daze, I heard something behind me. When I turned around there was Bill running down the hall behind me. Running! With an aneurism!

"Don't worry about me," he said. "Everything is going to be okay."

The next day as he was being transported, he accused the ambulance drivers of hitting every hole and bump in the road. At one point he woke up and the ambulance was parked at a convenient store/gas station. He looked around and the ambulance drivers were inside getting coffee and donuts. He put on a pair of boots in the back of the ambulance and went inside, too. When they saw him, they freaked out.

"What are you doing? You're not supposed to be in here!" they said.

He told them, "Neither are you! I want some coffee!"

They took him to the wrong hospital in the first place and the nurse hollered at them and said, "You can't leave him here! This is not the right hospital!"

They had to put him back in the ambulance and go to the big Duke University Hospital. When Misty and I finally got there, he said he had not been there much longer than we had.

The doctor at Duke said, "I don't normally see people like you. They are already in the graveyard."

My mind was filled with "What ifs." What if they hadn't found the aneurism? What if he hadn't got there in time? What if he didn't make it through the surgery? What if he never got to come home again?

Surgery lasted for over ten hours. My mind was a battlefield of worry and fear. All I could do was pray and know that others were, also.

They repaired the aneurism, replaced his heart valve, and did a bypass. Bill was in ICU for two or three days and all he would say was "Oh, baby!"

I thought he had suffered a stroke, but the doctor said it was because he was under the anesthesia for so long that his thoughts were still foggy. During that time, he had horrible flashbacks and hallucinations of Vietnam. Our daughter Misty and I promised to watch over him and then he would settle down and sleep.

On the fifth day, one of the nurses came into the room wearing a Duke shirt, but you couldn't see the D or E. Bill said, "I can't believe UK just came in through the door."

That marked a turning point. He started coming back to himself. The doctors would not give him any pain medicine except liquid Tylenol. Misty and I walked with him every day for therapy until he could walk a mile. He got to come home a week early.

I retired from the hospital to be with him at home and care for him. Five months later he passed away in his sleep. We had just celebrated our 48th wedding anniversary.

Bill would always say that he didn't like to say good-bye. He couldn't even tell his papaw goodbye. When God called him home, he went so fast that he couldn't tell me good-bye.

The morning after he died, all I could think or say was, "What am I going to do without him?"

I felt like my heart had been ripped out of my body, and only half had been put back in. How does a person go on without the one they have loved for over 50 years of life? All I could think was that I wish I could die and be with him.

Later in the day, I fell asleep. When I woke up, the Lord spoke to me and said, "I gave you five extra years with Bill."

I said, "Yes, Lord. You did."

When Bill had the aneurism in 2011, the doctor said the aneurism had cracked, bled, and sealed itself back together. That was highly unusual.

The Lord is near to those who have a broken heart and saves such as have a contrite spirit. (Psalm 34:18)

During the past year and a half, I have come to realize that Bill went the way he wanted to go. He didn't have to suffer for a long time or be taken care of (which would have caused him great grief to have to be taken care of hand and foot).

Every night I say, "It's you and me again tonight Lord," and I know He is. The Word of God promises that He will never leave me nor forsake me. He is always here with me.

It has been hard, learning to live without Bill, but God is still working on me to heal my broken heart and bring peace to my troubled thoughts. Each day, God strengthens me and helps me be victorious in that day. One day at a time, I am fighting the battle in my mind of life as a widow and making adjustments.

I still have things to work through, but my peace comes in knowing that when my battles on earth are completed, my victory is already won.

Have not I commanded thee? Be strong and of a good courage; be not afraid, neither be thou dismayed: for the Lord thy God is with thee whithersoever thou goest. *(Joshua 1:9 KJV)*

And the Lord, he it is that doth go before thee; he will be with thee, he will not fail thee, neither forsake thee: fear not, neither be dismayed. (Deuteronomy 31:8)

Being Spiritually Minded
Donna Price

"A person can get so spiritually minded, they are of no earthly good." I heard a minister say that recently in a sermon on CD. He could have included my name in that quote and been accurate.

Growing up in the home of a pastor, most of our lives were centered around the church. That included church activities, church responsibilities, church family, church expectations, and on and on. We were supposed to live our lives under a microscope so that no one could find fault in us. We were supposed to think about God and heaven and lost souls more than we thought about anything else.

I was expected to watch only certain TV shows, never go to the theater, listen to nothing but Christian music, have only Christian friends, dress a certain way, talk a certain way, behave a certain way, and dream about heaven and how to get there the rest of the time.

God spoke to my heart from the time I was a child. I talked to Him and on very special and very rare occasions, He spoke to me in a very clear voice. I had visions and dreams with spiritual significance about the plight of the human soul and eternity.

All these things were my "normal." I thought every true Christian lived like my family lived. Our church and faith were the center of my universe. I thought the rest of the world who didn't, needed to.

I loved God with all my heart as much as I knew how. I'd been a Christian since I was old enough to ask Jesus into my heart at age five or before. I went to sleep reading my Bible every night or praying for everyone I could think of who needed it. I even slept with a Bible under my pillow to keep bad dreams and vampires away. I fasted regularly.

I also wore a cross pendant all the time, just in case I met someone new who didn't know how much I loved Jesus. I wanted that to be the first and most important impression I made on anyone.

There were a few other kids in my life who were just like me, but not many. We were supposed to shine our lights for those who weren't like us to find their way to faith.

I was becoming a spiritual robot. I did not allow myself to be human. There was no room in my ideal of the perfect Christian for my flesh to have any part of my life.

Imagine my surprise when I went away to a Christian college and discovered that it was filled with young people and faculty who truly loved God, but they looked nothing like me. They also didn't think like me.

The girls wore pants, boys wore knee length shorts, and they all laughed a lot. They acted silly and seemed to be having a lot of fun. They liked themselves and each other.

I wasn't used to that. I was a very serious child and was becoming a stoic and serious adult. I had not been brought up to embrace my humanity. I was afraid to let myself be human.

If a human being could achieve perfection, I intended it to be me. I thought of myself like a Protestant nun. I had taken a vow of celibacy and given all my heart's desires to God. I was convinced that if I ever married it would be to a man who had made exactly the same vows. Our flesh would not be a problem because we would never have sex. I might have been living in an imperfect and fallen world, but I would never be part of it.

I quoted scriptures for every occasion and spoke Christianese fluently. I thought I had a firm grip on understanding the purpose of life and my place in it. I was special to God because I was such a good girl and always had been. The world couldn't touch me, or so I thought.

What really got my attention and struck the first brick out of place in my ivory tower was how much love flowed out of one particular girl that was very popular on campus.

She wore jeans and t-shirts and had shoulder length hair. She was always laughing and seemed to know everyone by name. In return, most students on campus seemed to know her and always seemed glad to see her.

I was curious about her because she absolutely did not fit into the mold of what I thought a Christian had to be. On the outside she was nothing like me.

I watched the way she interacted with people. It was genuine. She cared about people and it was obvious that she loved God, but it was in a whole different way than how I'd grown up.

When she invited me to attend a Christian function on campus, I went out of curiosity. She introduced me to several people and they all seemed to be genuinely caring and friendly. They didn't look like me or sound like me either. They seemed to be happy in a way I didn't know and laughed and enjoyed each other.

I continued to attend the gatherings. They talked about the joy of the Lord, which I realized soon enough that I didn't know much about. They talked about living "the abundant life," and I knew I didn't feel abundant in the same ways they did.

When they would join hands and stand in a circle to pray, I was confident that I would be good at that because I prayed all the time. But they didn't pray super spiritual sounding prayers and quote scripture while they prayed. They talked to God like He was a true friend who wanted to hear from them and who would answer.

I wasn't struggling with my faith in God, but I was struggling with trying to reconcile such drastically different approaches to God. Which one was right? Hadn't I always been right in my pursuit of God and His holiness?

One night the group had a campfire and was roasting hotdogs. They sang by the firelight about people knowing we are Christians by our love. The truth swept over me in a confusing wave of emotions.

It was their love that set them apart. They loved God, but they also loved each other. They genuinely cared about other people, other nations, other faiths. God's love was IN them.

The truth was staring at me. I loved God, absolutely. But I didn't love this sinful world. I didn't love people so easily who were not like me and didn't want to be.

I always went to God in prayer about everything, and I turned to my Bible. The answer was in the "Love Chapter."

"Though I speak with the tongues of men and of angels, but have not love, I have become sounding brass or a clanging cymbal. 2 And though I have the gift of prophecy, and understand all mysteries and all knowledge, and though I have all faith, so that I could remove mountains, but have not love, I am nothing. 3 And though I bestow all my goods to feed the poor, and though I give my body to be burned, but have not love, it profits me nothing.

4 Love suffers long and is kind; love does not envy; love does not parade itself, is not puffed up; 5 does not behave rudely, does not seek its own, is not provoked, thinks no evil; 6 does not rejoice in iniquity, but rejoices in the truth; 7 bears all things, believes all things, hopes all things, endures all things.

8 Love never fails. But whether there are prophecies, they will fail; whether there are tongues, they will cease; whether there is knowledge, it will vanish away. 9 For we know in part and we prophesy in part. 10 But when that which is perfect has come, then that which is in part will be done away.

[11] When I was a child, I spoke as a child, I understood as a child, I thought as a child; but when I became a man, I put away childish things. [12] For now we see in a mirror, dimly, but then face to face. Now I know in part, but then I shall know just as I also am known.

[13] And now abide faith, hope, love, these three; but the greatest of these is love." *(I Corinthians 13)*

All of my manufactured holiness did not impress God. My appearance may have appeased those who believed like me, but God saw past my outside cloaking straight into my heart. I wasn't wicked. I wasn't a fraud, but I also didn't realize just how much we are all sinners in need of a Sa"vior and all saved by grace through Christ. We are acceptable to God only because of our faith in Him, and not because of our own righteousness.

I didn't have to change any of the things about me that pleased my family or my church friends at home, but I did have to change my judgmental outlook on others who were not like me, and I did have to change my heart to love more than just God, my church, and my family.

When the minister made the statement that some people are so heavenly minded, they are of no earthly good, I knew exactly what he was talking about because I used to be one.

The stranger who dwells among you shall be to you as
[a]one born among you, and you shall love him as
yourself; for you were strangers in the land of Egypt: I
am the LORD your God. (Leviticus 19:34)

...be ye steadfast, unmovable, always abounding in the work of the Lord, forasmuch as ye know that your labor is not in vain in the Lord. (I Corinthians 15:58)

Yea, though I walk through the valley of the shadow of death, I will fear no evil: for thou art with me; thy rod and thy staff they comfort me. (Psalm 23:4)

My journey of Faith,
Learning to Trust in Jesus
Darla Shepherd

After twelve years of waiting patiently for a new beginning with a job opportunity, could it really be possible that I had two different job interviews within a week? Either would bring about complete career changes. Seeking the Lord for what seemed like a forever promise of a "Wonderful Job" was finally taking place!

At this point in my walk with the Lord I had been saved and faithfully serving Jesus for a little over six years. I had learned to trust Him for all of my needs, spiritually, mentally, emotionally, physically, financially, and with a career path. In the town where I come from, to say that jobs are scarce would be an understatement!

I knew it was my time to shine in a career change! I knew the opportunity was because I'd put my trust in Jesus. With Him being the Master of the Universe, I sometimes like to imagine Him enjoying showing off in the lives of His children! Ephesians 3:20 reminds us that He is able!

I was offered one of the positions and I felt as if my sanity depended on this change. With much prayer and fasting, I knew that I had made the right decision about what specific job I chose!

Finally, after background checks and tons of new hire paperwork were all out of the way I was ready to walk through the door of this new position. For the second time in thirteen years, I was excited to have a job with benefits offered, bonus checks that I never knew existed, and a work schedule with no Saturdays! I could hardly wait to begin a new mission field with new people to whom I could witness about Jesus! I would have a new doctor to work for and learn from. It was all mind blowing!

Over the next few weeks, everything was very new. Sad to say, I did not adapt to change as easily as I thought I would. My new job was overwhelming.

Why is it that the older a person gets it seems like it gets harder to adjust to change?

I soaked up everything like a sponge, taking notes, carrying a note pad in the back of my pocket jotting everything down constantly and consistently.

I remember thinking and even saying aloud, "The joy of the Lord is my strength." (Nehemiah 8:10)

It wasn't long before this job let me know it was not the easy God send I thought it was going to be. What it looked like on paper and what it was in reality were two different things.

Part of the problem was that we were thrown into our new positions without enough proper training. There was way more work than three people were able to do, and at times only two people were present to carry the load.

Everything was always changing. It never failed that every time I thought I was finally mastering it, the demands changed again. I suppose another hard adjustment was because I went from working part time three days a week to a full five-day week schedule that was way over booked, plus the promise of "no Saturdays" turned into working one Saturday a month.

I remember thinking, "*Lord use me for your glory,*" and trying to be determined that I was going to make it. Deep inside, I just did not know if I was going to or not.

Weeks became months. The original excitement quickly wore off. While pretending it was great for everyone else's sake, on the inside I knew that I missed the voice of the Lord.

Did I take the wrong job? Should I have never left my old one? I remember thinking, *"God what are you doing to me?"*

I was ashamed, scared, frustrated, overwhelmed, miserable, lonely, and discouraged. I tried to adopt the attitude that every day was a new day. I tried to be positive, encouraging, and show the love of Jesus. I knew my sole purpose was to try to show His love, be joyful, and sing praises (while I felt as if I was in a prison cell of silence).

It seemed to me that this workplace needed unity. Therefore, I usually carried devotion books, hoping someone might be interested. On my lunch break I would go pray, read my Bible, or listen to preaching in the break room.

I was learning something new every day, and I refused to give up! I had come too far. Failure was not an option.

I would tell myself, *"Suck it up butter cup"*, and *"What doesn't kill you will make you stronger."* I repeated those phrases on a daily basis. I quoted in my mind repeatedly, *"The joy of the Lord is my strength!"*

Life seemed so hard. Changing jobs was supposed to make our lives better – not worse! Work was a struggle. In the midst of this challenging job, home life was becoming tough. My husband seemed always to catch the raw end of the deal.

He dealt with me crying and screaming, "I hate it!" and wanting to give up every day. For the first six months I cried myself to sleep.

Have you ever found yourself in a place that you knew beyond any doubt that you had heard the voice of God? I surely thought I had after much prayer and seeking God about this change before I got the job.

The battle in my mind and spirit was that possibly I had made the wrong decision. Maybe I hadn't heard from God. Maybe I didn't know how to hear His voice. Maybe I was only fooling myself about being able to hear from God about the decisions in my life. The enemy highlighted and magnified my doubts and struggle. I felt like Paul with a thorn in my flesh, but I was the one who had created it.

I did conquer many giants. Slowly and surely, I got the hang of things and learned the new tasks. I hope to have also made some lifelong friends.

I tried every way possible to maintain character and integrity by showing the love of Jesus to those around me. Under the work stress the entire staff was under, I was trying to show joy that only God could bring, but I was going through the motions of saying and doing those things. I was not at peace and I was always trying to manufacture the joy I didn't always feel. I was trying to keep up a brave front.

Home life went on. Being a mother to a sweet little seven-year-old and a step mom to a seventeen-year-old boy as well, I needed my time at home not to be a reflection of the stress and challenges I had to face at work. Thank God, I was wife to a husband that refused to give up on me.

I knew the blessings of the Lord were all around, even though I was feeling forsaken in my job situation. My husband wanted me to quit.

He just wanted me happy! He knew I wasn't and my struggle was showing up in our home life. Our reality was that he had a job that meant he would be laid off in the winter months and I needed to work in order to cover those months. It was not that easy to quit and just walk away from a steady job no matter how much I wanted to!

Church life was always busy. I had accepted a position as leader of our church's Ladies Ministry. This involvement with our church helped keep me in check and occupied.

Few close friends knew that I was not happy with my job. They encouraged me when I was not able to encourage myself. Their prayers and support helped me keep my sanity. I stayed in my prayer closet and begged God to have his way, but in my heart, I needed him to move me. I needed Him to move me out of the job that I had though was His gift but was draining me.

In the meantime, I continued praying and fasting. I was so conflicted! It seemed selfish to ask God to move on my behalf again for another job opportunity. I couldn't quit without a different job in place because of our finances.

In time the answer came. Unbelievably, an amazing position opened, and I had a new job interview! A position had become available at a place I had never heard of before. Job duties consisted of a background that I was very familiar in the area of dental and vision health because of my previous job experiences.

Could it be possible?

My interview went great! It was blessed by God! As I walked out the door, I remember praying for the Lord to show me His mercy once again.

Finally, I had built up enough time in the old job to take a few days' vacation. I desperately needed to get a break away while I waited on the position announcement.

A small group of ladies decided to drive to Hamilton, Alabama for a Christian Ladies' Retreat. It was a change of scenery with a group of women I enjoyed spending time with. I hoped to be renewed and revived.

When we got there the theme was *Arise and Shine,* along with *Restoration.*

Chapter 30 of 1 Samuel tells the story of how King David's kingdom was invaded by an enemy army and the losses were incredible. The story goes on to tell how David went down and met the enemy in battle and recovered all that had been lost.

The conference and this story in particular were the inspiration I needed. I took the message to heart. *"You will surely recover everything that was taken from you."* I believed it was all God ordained in the heavenly realm for me to be there at the conference and hear this encouraging message.

The very last night during worship I heard, the Lord say *"Trust,"* which was the key to my breakthrough.

The Holy Spirit revealed to me that I had lost trust in my Savior. The battle that had been raging in my mind about the job situation and whether I had heard God or not when I changed jobs wasn't as much about the positions as it was about my trust in the One who never fails.

In the midst of what seemed like thirteen years of hard job situations, that year of battling with my unhappiness had just about killed me emotionally and spiritually. I had slipped into such a dark place of silence and desperation.

I was also under guilt and condemnation for not having all of my issues worked out. I was working in church, and directing Women's Ministries, so how could I feel so desperate and alone? Where was my faith? I was supposed to be the one who was leading other women to a closer relationship with God while my own was slipping. I was a mess!

I felt as if a leader should never show weakness. So, I tried never to do that. I put on my mask of smiles and a happy face, trying to look like what I thought a leader should look like. Of course, all of these battles in my mind were tricks of the enemy. He wanted me to quit, give up, have a nervous breakdown and die. I knew how good God had been to me in my life but felt so forsaken because of the unhappy job situation.

The Holy Spirit emphasized this scripture to me, "Trust in the LORD with all your heart, And lean not on your own understanding; In all your ways acknowledge Him, And He shall [a]direct your paths. (Proverbs 3:5-6 NKJV)

Trust in the Lord with all your heart. I fell to my face and began to ask the Lord to forgive me for my lack of faith and trust. I asked Him to cleanse me from all crazy emotions that I had felt over the past year.

Repentance is good for the soul! The love of Jesus washed me clean and the Holy Spirit comforted me. I felt a great weight lift from my heart and mind.

I acknowledged Him and knew He would direct my path. If He wanted me to stay put, I would stay, no matter the cost. He had a purpose even if I couldn't see it.

I felt a release in the spirit. The word of God says in John 8:36 "Therefore if the Son makes you free, you shall be free indeed."

Things had changed in the realm of the spirit. Restoration was taking place! I knew it was for me. Like Abraham, I began to "call things as though they were."

My sisters in Christ did the same for their own lives and personal needs. The entire trip home we spoke faith into existence that the job was mine! I began to prepare for it.

When I got home I received a phone call from a new (soon to be) supervisor that said, "Darla, I prayed and ask the Lord to send someone that would have a heart for the people and I believe that it is you!"

I prayed and knew the Lord had moved once again on my behalf! It was time for my wonderful new position to unfold! After giving a two-week notice, I started my new job on the one-year anniversary date from the job I was leaving. I had endured for one year, but it had seemed like a lifetime.

Looking back now after just celebrating one year being at my "God job" as like to call it, I cannot help but cry and thank my Lord and Savior for being so faithful! He keeps his promises.

2 Chronicles 20:15 says, "Thus says the Lord to you: Do not be afraid nor dismayed because of this great multitude, for the battle is not yours, but God's."

Looking back, I realize that we serve a Savior who dots his i's and crosses his t's! My job incorporates everything and more that I have learned from thirteen years of job experience and background work history. All of it trained me and prepared me for the position I currently have.

I could go on for days telling how much I love my position and all of the ways I serve the community through work. I can't thank God enough for this radical, important change in my life that has truly restored my joy.

Allow the joy of the Lord to be your strength no matter the struggle in your journey! Trust Him! Rest assured that God is good! Most importantly do not ever lose faith in your journey of learning to trust in Jesus!

And we know that in all things works together for good to those who love God, to those who are called according to His purpose. (Romans 8:28 NKJV)

If God be for us, who can be against us? (Romans 8:31 KJV)

Casting down imaginations, and every high thing that exalteth itself against the knowledge of God, and bringing into captivity every thought to the obedience of Christ. (2 Corinthians 10:5)

Thank God for a Broken Engagement

Anonymous

Some girls dream of marrying a handsome prince. I dreamed of marrying a minister. It didn't matter is he was tall and handsome, short and round, bald, or hairy. Having committed his life to the call of God to serve in ministry was the most important quality any man could have in my mind. I loved and wanted to serve God with all of my heart. I was positive that God had created me for that purpose alone – to be the wife of a minister and work beside of him.

It didn't matter if he felt called to be a pastor, an evangelist, or a missionary. He just had to be "called". My parents were strongly devoted to their church and their denomination. Imagine their joy when I became engaged to a young man who was studying for the ministry in their own denomination. Surely it was a match made in heaven!

I accepted the proposal, believing it was part of my divine destiny. It would be a holy union, an anointed marriage, a joint commission in which we both served God with all our hearts. Our children would be beautiful, well behaved, intelligent examples of what a minister's wife, family, and children should be.

I had it all blissfully worked out in my mind. I was so happy with my dream for the future and so excited that it was coming true. It didn't hurt that my fiancé was tall and gorgeous, either. Other girls wanted to be me. It was great knowing that everyone thought we were the perfect match.

I was in my last year as a teenager and had been under the authority of my father and mother as I grew up. I was used to letting people tell me what to do. When my fiancé started telling me how long to wear my skirts and choosing clothes that "were suitable for a pastor's wife," how long to wear my hair, and how much jewelry and make-up I could or couldn't wear it seemed like he had the right to do that. After all, he was a man of God and was going to be my husband. I would submit to him in all things.

It wasn't like I hadn't had other boyfriends. I had fallen in love (I thought) more than once in my young years. There was one young man that I couldn't stop thinking about, but he was not a minister.

The closer it got to the wedding, the less sure I was of anything. My fiancé was a holy man in front of everyone, but when we were alone together, he was just a man. When I began to feel convicted about our prolonged hugging, kissing, and "petting" sessions, he would assure me that I belonged to him and we were already committed to each other. Marriage was just a formality. But in my heart, I knew something wasn't right. I wanted to wait another year before we got married. I didn't want to be a teen bride. BUT, I was afraid we could not control our passion for each other if we didn't go ahead and marry.

He became more jealous the closer we got to the wedding and the more controlling. He didn't want me to speak to anyone without his permission it seemed. When I asked if he didn't trust me, he said it was all the other men out there that he didn't trust.

As he tried to tighten his control, something inside of me started pushing back. My dream had cracks in it, but I wasn't willing to admit it to anyone at first, including myself.

With the wedding a few months away, I was making myself sick with worry, but had no one to talk to. When I tried to talk to my fiancé about how young I was and my dreams of completing college, he seemed to always say the right things, but I was not comforted by his words. I started questioning God about it.

The truth was, I had prayed a generic prayer listing my desires in a husband and a future, but I don't remember ever asking God if this young man was the right young man. Because he was the available young man who was asking and fit the characteristics of the man in my dreams, I suppose I assumed that was God's answer.

There were other ministers out there looking for wives. What if I had said yes to the wrong one? When I was honest with myself, I wasn't sure if I was truly in love with him, or if I was just in love with the dream I had created surrounding him. Honestly, I liked everyone's reaction to the fact that I was the one this young minister had chosen to be his bride. I enjoyed the attention.

My anxieties mounted and when I tried to talk to my mom about it, she told me that I was just getting wedding jitters. "Cold feet" were normal, she said. She had always been wild about my dad and she said even she got a little nervous before their wedding.

My dad had a college degree and so did she. They had waited until they were finished with their college studies to get married. Part of me wanted that experience, but I wanted to marry a minister more than even that.

This did not relieve my growing doubts and fears. Even if we were meant for each other, did we have to get married when I was so young? If he really loved me, wouldn't he be willing to wait until we were both sure about the timing? I started wondering if he truly loved me, or if he was racing toward a legal union in which he would be entitled to sex on demand. He was very happy with the fact that I was a virgin and he would be the only man I ever knew.

I was afraid of the whole concept of becoming "one flesh." In those days, a young woman was supposed to figure things out AFTER she was married, with very little or no instruction about what to expect from anyone. I had stumbled upon private conversations about marriage and sex, but people clammed up around me on this subject. I was afraid to ask questions and too dumb to even know what to ask.

Less than a month before the wedding, I broke the engagement. I couldn't sleep, and I couldn't keep food down. Guilt and doubt constantly invaded my thoughts. It was the biggest battle in my mind that I had ever faced in my young life. I told him I wanted to marry him, but I wanted to wait. He argued that it didn't make sense to wait and what would everyone think?

He was used to sweet talking me into anything he really wanted and using his faith to back it up, and I was used to letting him because he was a godly man and would be the head of our home. When I resisted him in this one thing, the timing of the wedding, he became furious with me.

He screamed and yelled, stomped around, and looked like he wanted to hurt me. The raving lunatic in front of me was NOT the man I thought I was going to marry. He told me I was a ruined woman and no other man would ever want his leftovers, especially not a minister. He threatened to tell everyone what kind of girl I really was.

As if his fury wasn't enough, my mother was furious as well. Shower invitations were out. Some wedding gifts had come in. Wedding invitations were already in the mail and most of the plans had been finalized. Considerable expenses had already been accumulated. Her fury with me was almost equal to that of my lost love.

My dad on the other hand said he was relieved and that I shouldn't marry any man if I didn't truly love him, preacher or not. He never mentioned the money that had already been lost on wedding arrangements.

My mind was flooded with doubts, lost dreams, and above all that turmoil, the voice of the enemy continually told me what an idiot I was. I was a loser. I had thrown away my dreams for nothing more than fear and doubt.

For years I chastised myself. I suffered reproach from my church family, and snickers from my friends. By the age of 27, I was turning into an old maid. Maybe that's what I deserved.

My former fiancé found true love in a very short amount of time and married quickly. He was settled in as pastor of a mid-sized church a couple of hours away. He was happy and living the dream without me in it. I couldn't help wondering what kind of girl he married.

I did not want to be single. I doubted myself. I doubted my dreams. I doubted God's opinion of me. I doubted the future. I doubted that my dreams would ever come true. There was a constant battle in my mind, but I clung to God desperately. I wanted Him to accept me and love me more than anyone else.

I let go of my childish dreams, and started standing on the verse, *"In all they ways acknowledge Him, and He will direct your paths."* If God meant for me to spend my life alone and serve him alone, that was going to be okay. Other women did it all the time.

I had accepted the possibility of singleness. I wasn't looking for a handsome prince or a handsome minister. I just wasn't looking period. I had a good job and a steady paycheck. I had my own little place in the world with friends and family who loved me. That would have to be enough. I enjoyed my freedom and was beginning to feel like an independent woman.

Little did I know that the young man I hadn't been able to forget when I was engaged was still single and our paths were destined to cross at a Christian conference. He was as surprised to see me as I was to see him. He had assumed that I did go through with the marriage. Our paths had been in different directions for a long time.

We went out to "catch up" and began to see each other more frequently. When we started dating, I was amazed that he didn't try to rule everything about me.

When he asked me to marry him, I did not hesitate about saying "yes" or setting a date. We've been married for over 30 years, and pastor a local community church. He treats me as his equal and regards me as a co-laborer in Christ, called to serve together. He is my handsome prince, best friend, blessing, rock, and the best thing God knew I needed. I respect him in all things. I appreciate that he lets me be me and has never tried to turn me into someone I wouldn't even recognize in the mirror.

Dad always said he just wanted me to be happy. Mother finally came around. My true friends rejoiced with me that God had saved the best for a future appointment instead of me settling for what was convenient and available when I was young.

I wasn't ready for all the responsibilities of being a wife, and especially a pastor's wife as a teenager. God knew that. In those years of doubt in between, He was growing me up, teaching me, and preparing me for my dreams and the desires of my heart when He brought them to me in His time and when I was mature enough to appreciate them.

Sometimes we struggle with balancing our dreams and desires with reality. We want what we want when we want it and we don't want to have to wait for anything, but God's timing is perfect. His plan for us is always better than our plan for ourselves. If we ask Him to direct our paths, He will be ordering our steps even when we don't realize it.

Thank God for a broken engagement!

Watch ye, stand fast in the faith, quit you like men, be strong. (I Corinthians 16:13 KJV)

Perfectionism

Brenda Boyens Correll

My dad went into full-time ministry when I was quite young. Being a minister's child contributed a lot to my way of thinking. I was raised in a culture where the minister and his family were held to a much higher standard than those in their congregation, especially morally. These expectations, at times very unreasonable, resulted in me embracing a mindset of "perfectionism".

I started to hold myself accountable to a higher standard concerning behavior, academics, actions, and speech. It may sound really good, but subconsciously it fostered various fears that handicapped and enslaved me.

Thinking back over my life, I realize that I missed out on so many great experiences as a kid, for example: jet skiing, rock climbing, scuba diving etc. My fears were ridiculous and unfounded. I would not try something completely new, because I was too afraid that I would not get it right the first time. I was a prisoner to the fear of failure.

The truth was that I did not realize that I was plagued and emotionally handicapped by fear. I knew that I struggled with perfectionism, but the label or mask of perfectionism covered and concealed the true culprit - FEAR. I was afraid of failure. I was afraid of disappointing those around me if I didn't live up to expectations set for me.

I managed to control and structure my life in such a manner that I did not have to deal with uncertainties for the most part. I travelled to various countries and even worked abroad, totally clueless that I had been deceived and therefore did not recognize my own handicaps and fears. Fortunately, we serve a God who constantly transforms and renews us.

Perfectionism was not my only hang-up. God in His wisdom helped me throughout my life to deal with and demolish other mental strongholds and addictive behaviors, as well. Many were born from being a pastor's daughter who was expected to be perfect in all ways.

Finally, in my 40's, it was time to look perfectionism in the eye and deal with its root cause. By then I was married and my husband, a psycho therapist, had his own struggles with perfectionism. It was a first-time marriage for both of us and the adjustments were relatively easy. Since we did not have any kids of our own, we decided to become foster parents to sibling groups in order to prevent them from being split up and sent individually to different foster homes.

Our first placement was a sibling group of five during summer vacation. It would have been funny if it had not been so totally overwhelming. My experience as a teacher could not in any way, shape, or manner prepare me for this transition. I was in tears the very first evening, but quitting was not an option. There was no way to be prepared for every possible scenario! God knew I had to be thrown into the deep end so that I could recognize my fears for what they really were.

Perfectionism was exposed for what it really was: the fear of not knowing exactly how to handle a new challenge successfully! Throughout my life, I had not allowed myself the grace of a learning curve. It is easier to conquer struggles we face when we can identify them and expose the lies for what they really are.

I dealt with an avalanche of first time experiences since I had no framework or file to mentally access. The health check-ups, documentations, challenging behaviors, school enrollment and going from two adults to a family of seven overnight are just a few of the difficulties I had to face for the first time. The icing on the cake was that we did not have all the information we needed at times. "I do not know," became a common response.

There was not enough time to plan or figure it out. I had to learn to deal with situations on the spot and not to allow feelings of anxiety or frustrations to overwhelm me. My husband and I did not only survive this four-and-a-half-month ordeal, but we embarked on in a journey of greater healing and freedom ourselves.

I wish I could say that God set us quickly and completely free from our various fears, but that was not the case.

Next, we took in a sibling group of four kids and ended up adopting three of them. This time around was easier in some regards and much more challenging in others. Our journey to adopt played another pivotal part in our healing, recovery, and transformation. This time the kids would become ours forever, instead of returning home.

The neat thing about kids is that they are very forgiving and do not harbor grudges indefinitely. They lovingly, and patiently afford us many "do-over" opportunities. They do not expect us to be perfect just as we do not expect them to be so. During the last five years we have grown together and as individuals. Unconditional love is still something we strive to uphold, since love is the greatest antidote for fear.

Our kids are facing their own battles with fear that they came honestly by, due to their childhood experiences. They have embraced lying as a means of protecting themselves from punishment before entering our home. After trying various methods to encourage them to always tell the truth, we are focusing on healing of the soul, which includes the heart, mind and will.

We realize we need greater revelations of God's love for us all. Our hearts play a cardinal role in our ability to overcome challenges and be transformed into his likeness.

An older Vineyard hymn has become one of our favorite bedtime songs. The words speak of a changed heart and a desire to be like God.

We are all committed to the process of transforming our minds and renewing our souls. Prayer and The Word of God are central on our journey to greater freedom. We rejoice at every victory and are so thankful for the liberty and freedom we currently experience.

My journey has become our family's journey. It is both a joy and a privilege to share this adventure including its hiccups and breakthroughs with my loving family. The victories are greater, and the struggles are lighter, since they are shared. Breaking free from the bondage of perfectionism has released me to experience greater joy, deeper love, patience, and truly be transformed by the renewing of my mind.

Brenda Boyens Correll

You crown the year with Your goodness, And Your paths drip with abundance. (Psalm 65:11 NKJV)

The Lord shall fight for you, and you shall hold your peace. (Exodus 14:14)

The Spirit of Heaviness: (depression, oppression, weariness, despondency)

Rhonda Long Robinson

To appoint unto them that mourn in Zion, to give unto them beauty for ashes, the oil of joy for mourning, the garment of praise for the spirit of heaviness... (Isaiah 61:3)

"Is this it?"

My mind goes back to that day in 1996. I asked myself this question as the doctor handed me a slip of paper. I was upset. I wanted answers to why at 36 years of age I was feeling drained and tired all the time. I reluctantly and slowly reached out and took the slip of paper.

In dismay I asked, "What is this?" He began to tell me that the reason I was tired, was that I was depressed. He acted confused when I had replied, "No" when he asks me if anyone in my family was on antidepressants.

"You mean to tell me no one in your family takes antidepressants?" he said in disbelief.

I had not come into my current position as a clinical counselor at that time, but I knew enough to ask myself some questions. He had not done a psychosocial evaluation on me that would have revealed the environmental factors that could be contributing to my issues. There were trying circumstances going on in my life beyond my control that would only take time to resolve.

At that time, I was a high school art teacher. In the middle of the day I found myself turning off the lights, locking my door, and laying down behind my desk. I knew something was wrong. I had always been very active as a girl and remained so as an adult. I loved to be outside, hiking, kayaking, horseback riding, working in my garden, or anything to do with the outdoors.

In regard to my work, I had always been driven to be my best. Suddenly I found myself walking in a "fog." I had a hard time focusing. I could not sleep. I would even get up in the middle of the night and start walking outside.

I found myself in a state of despondency. My mental state was in much turmoil. I would sit outside on my steps in the middle of the night begging God to help me.

As tears flowed, I told God that everything in my life was suffering, my work, my personal life, and my family. I did not know if this had something to do with my hormones or a spiritual attack. As it turned out, it was both.

My motivation was gone. I was no longer active in any of the things that usually brought me joy. My work was suffering. I remember one day going into my little back office that had no windows into the pitch dark. I got down on my knees and buried my face into my hands on the floor and begged God to help me get through the day.

I was not happy with myself, I knew I could do better, I had always been a go-getter, doing my personal best. I did not want to be this way but could not seem to help myself.

So, there I sat in the doctor's office asking myself, "Is this it?"

Thankfully by what I believe to be Divine intervention, I took my blood results to a nutritionist. I remember her words vividly.

"Did you not feel like you were about to pass out?" she asked in what almost seemed like shock as she read the results of my bloodwork. She went on to tell me that my blood sugar level was 40.

This made me very angry. What the doctor had been offering me would not have fixed the root of my distress. The physical imbalances were a clear answer to part of my issues.

Now as a clinical counselor, I base my practice on this principle, "You are only as healthy mentally as you are physically and spiritually."

The bloodwork also revealed that I had a vitamin B-12 and D deficiency, and my thyroid levels were low. All these deficiencies have the same symptoms as those manifested with depression. I started taking B-12 shots, vitamin D, and medication for thyroid imbalance.

I read somewhere that as women, we are prone to the attack of the enemy and vulnerable due to females being more in tune with the emotional side of the right brain. We feel emotions deeply.

I was attacked in my personal life as well. I was still reeling from the devastating impact on my family due to of the death of my mother, who had died from Lou Gehrig's disease six years previously. My dad's life seemed to go off the deep end, as I slowly watched him be drawn into the seductive world of women and drugs.

My precious 15-year-old daughter was under attack of the enemy, also. I seemed to be getting hit with overwhelming issues from every side. This was a spiritual battle that was only going to be won in that realm.

Through my tears, I cried out to God please help me. "I want you to get the glory out of this, and my life."

I recalled a dream my mother had told me when I was a teenager. She said she dreamed a giant and a midget were following her. One's name was Depression and the other's name was Oppression. The only way she could get rid of them was to rebuke them in the name of Jesus. When she did they began to shrink. That did not impact me at the time she told me. I hadn't been fully able to understand the importance of the dream, but it sure made sense to me while I was fighting this darkness.

The ladies at our church had been studying Beth Moore's Bible study, *Breaking Free.* In this study, we learned about generational curses.

Deuteronomy 5:9 states, "Thou shalt not bow down thyself unto them, nor serve them; for I, the Lord thy God, am a jealous God, visiting the iniquity of the fathers upon the children unto the third and fourth generation of them that hate Me."

I paid attention to the word "visit." This does not mean that we are predestined to be what our parents are, but we will be visited by temptation to follow their behaviors, which means we have the choice to open that door or keep it closed.

I found myself battling a spirit of heaviness that was crushing. I began to rebuke it in Jesus name. I was trying to do for myself what I could to take care of me and fight the spiritual battle I was in.

I was having a discussion with my Aunt Lilly on this subject not long ago. she asked me a question that brought even more light to my battle with this spirit. She asked me if I had known that my grandmother had been institutionalized at one time (when my mother was a little girl).

I thought, "Well, that explains a lot!"

I look back over the last thirteen years since I began this battle with the spirit of heaviness. I see how God delivered me and has sustained me.

Every so often, I found myself resisting this "depression", until about six months ago when a dear Christian woman called me out of the blue with a message. She told me she had been standing at her sink doing dishes. As she looked out the window, she had thoughts of me.

She said the Lord spoke to her and said, "Tell Rhonda, her giant is coming down."

The same giant that had been following my grandmother and mother, was trying to overshadow me. I was determined that it would be defeated in me and my generation, so my daughter and granddaughter would not have to fight it.

Two years ago, my daughter Jami came through the living room and I saw a very familiar look on her face, one that I had seen in my own. It was a face I remember from my childhood of my beautiful grandmother, who was there, but not there.

Jami looked at me with so much sadness in her eyes. It was a sadness I could not bear to see. She said, "Mommy I can't do this."

She was on her way to work. The heaviness was apparent all over her. Spiritual authority rose up in me and a cry of warfare in prayer. As she left for work, I grabbed my copy of *Power of a Praying Parent* by Stormy Omartain and marched up to her room. There I began to fight like I have never fought for her before in prayer. It was not just me that had been fighting the battle of depression, but my daughter had been as well. I declared in the name of Jesus, that the enemy would have to get his filthy hands of my daughter.

I have fought this battle of the mind, body, and spirit, and declared it won in the name of Jesus. It will not be passed down to my offspring!

My daughter came back home, and something had changed in her by the end of the day. I could see in her countenance that the spirit of heaviness had lifted from her.

Now in private practice, I encourage my clients who come in with symptoms of depression to go get a complete metabolic panel to see where any deficiencies may be and what their hormonal levels are. We address nutrition and physical activities that help stimulate the chemical dopamine which is secreted in the prefrontal cortex of the brain.

Dopamine gives us a sense of well-being. It is depleted by stress, mood altering substances, and an unhealthy lifestyle (lack of exercise and eating junk food). After this evaluation, we work on managing stress due to environmental circumstances. Finally, we address the spiritual components of which they may be under attack.

Those dark days long ago are still fresh in my memory. I am comforted in knowing that when God found me sitting in darkness and in the shadow of death, He delivered me when I cried out to Him.

Because of where I've been, I am better equipped to help those I encounter who are facing the battle with the spirit of heaviness. Our Heavenly Father does not intend for us to live in darkness and the shadow of death. He desires that we have peace, His peace that surpasses all understanding.

Luke 1:78 describes God's intervention for those who call on Him for help perfectly:

"Through the tender mercy of our God; whereby the dayspring from on high has visited us, 79To give light to them that sit in darkness and in the shadow of death, to guide our feet into the way of peace." (KJV)

Rhonda Long Robinson

The Lord will give strength unto His people, the Lord will bless His people with peace. (Psalm 29:11 KJV)

Open Doors
Judith Victoria Hensley

The telephone rang and the unexpected voice on the other end of the telephone was Dr. J.M. Boswell, the president of the college from which I had gotten my undergraduate degree in Religious Education and Biology. Even though I had been praying and asking God for direction and open doors in my life to lead me into the future, I could not have imagined God's hand at work in such an incredible way in my behalf.

He went straight to the point, "I understand you are interested in pursuing a teaching certificate."

"Yes, sir."

"Are you interested in returning to Williamsburg to do the necessary classwork?"

"Yes, sir, I am. But I have no money to pay for tuition."

I had been away from campus and married for six years, working at the University of Kentucky. It was incredible that this man remembered my name and actually cared about my situation. I had gone back to my parents' home in Illinois that summer, trying to get my bearings and figure out what I should do next, if the divorce actually went through.

"I understand you have a small child that will be accompanying you..."

"Yes, sir. He's 15 months old."

"Do you have a place to stay in Williamsburg?" he asked.

"I think I do temporarily..."

"Then it's settled. You come on down and fill out the paperwork. We'll find a position for you on campus. First Baptist Church has an excellent daycare program. I'm sure someone can help you find a place to live."

That conversation took place almost forty years ago. I may not recall it word for word and I'm sure it was a bit longer, but I will never forget God's miraculous intervention in my life. I had fasted and prayed off and on all summer for a total of thirty days immediately after an unexpected announcement that my husband was filing for divorce.

I cried out in desperation, and God heard my prayers. I begged God to send my husband back to us, to make the bad dream go away. I begged God to get his attention and shake him until his teeth rattled for making what I believed was a terrible mistake. That prayer wasn't answered, but God touched the heart of a college president on my behalf and opened doors for me that I could not have opened for myself.

Family and friends thought I was crazy to attempt such a thing. How in the world could I go back to school and take care of a baby? My parents wanted me to stay with them and my mother had volunteered to babysit while I found a job and worked there and went back to school. Jobs were plentiful in the Chicago suburb. There was a college nearby. It made perfect sense to stay with them for a season.

However, God had opened a door and I was determined to walk through it. Even with the divorce decree pending, no one could dissuade me that I had heard from God. I didn't know how things were going to turn out, but I knew with my whole heart that God was directing my paths.

I fought many battles of fear about trying to do it all on my own. I was certain that God would not lead me in a direction where He did not have a plan.

I finally convinced my parents and friends that I had to go. I had to try. If I fell flat on my face and couldn't make it, I promised to let them know.

I stayed with a family in the area for the first few weeks until I found an apartment. It was a little house detached from the main house that had once been a garage and had been converted to a rental property. It was perfect for baby and me. And it was right in the center of campus as part of a rare private residency that hadn't been bought up by the college.

The divorce was finalized. I was devastated but had plenty of other things on which to focus. I was not a quitter, and I would not let the circumstances defeat me. My heart was broken, and I fought a raging battle in my mind over and over about what had happened and why, and how things could have turned out differently. It was a never-ending gopher wheel that I could not stop racing on.

I worked three part time jobs. Two of them allowed me to bring my son with me in the evenings and on week-ends while I worked. During my classes and campus job, he was happily established in day care.

I completed my education classes, did student teaching, and was ready to face the world in much less than the projected time table. I loved the town and countryside. I did not want to pull up roots and start over again so soon, but God had other plans.

I lost all three jobs in less than two weeks. The dean of women decided my son was getting too old to be with me as a substitute dorm mother on week-ends and be exposed to so many girls running around in pajamas at night, etc. The young lady I had been babysitting had reached the age where her parents no longer thought she needed a babysitter. My campus office job ended when my classes ended.

Once again, it seemed as if my world was crashing down. What in the world was I going to do? Did God have a plan for me? Was I being punished for some unknown reason or shortcoming? Was I supposed to return to my parents' home 500 miles away? I was a bundle of success and failure all at the same time and I was totally confused.

A cousin reached out to me and said she had talked to the superintendent of schools where she lived and the director of special education. If I was willing to pick up three summer classes in special education, I would have a job waiting in the fall in my own classroom.

I placed the appropriate phone calls, made connections, filled out paperwork, took the classes, and began teaching in the fall in a unit of severely challenged students. The three courses I had taken that summer had in no way prepared me for such a diverse classroom of needs. I felt so inadequate. I knew I wasn't the best woman for the job.

I could not try to teach the children by day and forget about them at night. Their needs and limitations overwhelmed me, and I was consumed with them day and night.

Had God opened the door for me? If He had, shouldn't I have been happier? Shouldn't I have been better at it? I felt like a fraud.

I continued taking classes until I got the necessary certification in Special Education and taught for three years in that same demanding classroom. I was at the end of my rope. I cared very much about the children, but no matter how hard I worked, there were some limitations neither they nor I was not able to overcome.

Three years with the same students had not significantly changed the projected outcome for their futures. I was very discouraged. I felt like an utter failure.

I prayed and begged God to put me somewhere that I could see significant progress in my students. I needed to feel as if I was making a difference through my career choice.

When a teacher in my school retired because of health issues, the principal offered the job to me. He certainly didn't have to ask twice.

Work with first grade children was pure joy. I could see their progress steadily from the beginning of the year when they were non-readers to the end of the year when they were reading stories and books. They were counting and doing simple math problems. They loved to sing and have story time. They loved the adventure of school and they loved me as much as I fell in love with each class.

This small snapshot of my life story is certainly not meant to imply that there were not other struggles and challenges all along the way, but God was with me. He sustained me. He guided and directed me and gave me peace.

When a decision in my life must be made and I don't know what to do, I look for the peace of God and the open door. That combination never fails.

Judith Victoria Hensley

The four and twenty elders fall down before him that sat on the throne, and worship him that liveth for ever and ever, and cast their crowns before the throne... (Revelation 4:10)

The Battlefront
SLP

There are challenges in every life which we must overcome. The biggest challenge in my life so far as a woman, nurturer, caregiver, lover of good, warrior, truth weeker, encourager and exhorter is to allow God's truth to prevail in every circumstance.

I am a person who is used to being in charge in my career and making tough decisions. Sometimes that spills over into my personal life in personal decisions. It also spills over into my spiritual life when I take charge rather than seeking God and His truth. I have a strong will and a mind of my own. This arena of the mind is where my battles are fought.

Still, I desire God's truth in any and all given ideas and situations in my life. I want His truth to be the determining factor of my decision-making processes. I struggle with surrendering my own will to His.

I want to RENEW my thinking, and to walk out His truth and directions for my life. There are often struggles in my thought processes that get in the way. It is my desire to know and follow His leading regardless of what "I" want to focus on, yet, like Paul, I often fail.

The Apostle Paul wrote in his letter to the Roman church:

"For what I am doing, I do not understand. For what I will to do, that I do not practice; but what I hate, that I do. **16** If, then, I do what I will not to do, I agree with the law that it is good. **17** But now, it is no longer I who do it, but sin that dwells in me. **18** For I know that in me (that is, in my flesh) nothing good dwells; for to will is present with me, but how to perform what is good I do not find. **19** For the good that I will to do, I do not do; but the evil I will not to do, that I practice. **20** Now if I do what I will not to do, it is no longer I who do it, but sin that dwells in me." (Romans 7:15-20 *NKJV*)

I want His thoughts to be my thoughts in spite of what "I" want to think about any given situation. I want to trust in God's wisdom more than my own tendency to analyze and problem solve on my own. I struggle with slowing down long enough to listen to what God might be trying to say to me.

I want to be led by the Holy Spirit rather than following my emotions and feelings but struggle to do so. I want to hear God's voice above the clamor of my own logic and the advice of others. I don't want to be ensnared by "religious ways" that often find a stronghold inside the church.

I want to follow God even when it may hurt, even when I am afraid of having my heart hurt, or my mind. It isn't easy taking my hands off of things when I feel as if I know what should be done and how things should be done. I want to rise up so that I will follow God's leading despite what doing so might look like in the natural. I have to remind myself that I can't see the whole big picture like God does.

In the book of I Corinthians, Paul demonstrates this by comparing what we see and think we understand about what is going on around to looking through a dark glass and trying to see. We just can't do it.

God sees clearly, always. The things we don't understand now, we will one day see clearly. I don't have a clue about what is in my Father's mind for me or His far-reaching plans for my future, except the parts He allows me to see.

I am being refined in the fires of hard and severe times. Overcoming difficulties strengthens me, shapes me, and empowers me. There are times when following God's plan instead of my own seems like a loss, but in reality, there is gain! I've made choices that seemed like they were the hardest thing I've ever done to follow God instead of my heart, but there was satisfaction in knowing that I chose what I knew would most please the Lord.

In the twenty years I have walked with Jesus as my Lord and Savior, I have faced many battles in life. They are usually fought first on the battlefront of my mind. The greatest travesties of my life with The Lord so far, have been when I didn't allow Him to be the director of my thoughts and actions while I was going through both the good and the bad. By presuming that I knew "better" than what He was actually saying, based on Christian culture's opinion instead of looking at the harder truths of what He was "really" saying, I have created many problems for myself.

By using sacrifice as a substitute for obedience and deceiving myself that being "good" would pass His test, I have had to fight unnecessary battles and experienced unnecessary losses. How wrong I was. Obedience is better than sacrifice. When I surrender to His ways instead of mine or the culture's ways; when I say, "YES!" and align my mind and actions to take the steps needed to walk out His directives, the victory is powerful!

My prayer for all of us as women warriors of the faith is that we will become an army of believers who are willing to surrender all! As we surrender our will, trust Him for our desires, submit our thoughts and ways, we will pick up His instead, and walk in the kingdom of His power.

With our Lord's help, we (as sisters in Christ) all walk this walk together. As believers and members of the body of Christ, we can become one in mind and spirit. As women, we can rise higher into new heights as we seek a relationship with the King of Glory.

We are destined to be victorious! We are more than conquerors. He has called to each of us individually to fulfill our purpose for which He has created us. If we follow Him, we are destined to be victorious!

Be strong in the Lord and the power of His might.
(Ephesians 6:10 KJV)

Seek the LORD and his strength, seek his face continually. (I Chronicles 16:11)

The God of my rock; in him will I trust: he is my shield, and the horn of my salvation, my high tower, and my refuge, my saviour; thou savest me from violence. (II Samuel 22:3)

Jail Ministry
Judy Ball

I gave my heart to Jesus when I was a young girl in grade school. From that day forward, I was forever changed. I wanted to work for God. I wanted to be involved in some type of ministry.

Jail ministry was always something in my mind that I wanted to do, but I was busy raising a family, going to church, and my hands were full. After my husband went home to be with the Lord, I was left raising four children between the ages of three and thirteen. Alone and overwhelmed, I didn't leave much time for anything extra besides church. Thoughts of jail ministry or being active in any kind of ministry seemed unrealistic and out of reach.

I was blessed to sit under the preaching of a wonderful pastor, Bro. Thea Carter and his wife, Thelma Carter. I feel like she was my spiritual mother who taught me many things about serving God. Now at the age of 55, I am still holding onto my faith in Jesus and the part they played in my young years is part of my foundation.

There were ladies in that church who I watched for years who were involved in jail ministry. I was so disappointed that I couldn't be part of it.

My friend always reassured me and said, "Oh Judy, your children won't always be little. Your day will come, and you will get to go."

My heart yearned to go. I dreamed about going and sharing the love of God and His word to those who were in need.

My desire to serve and not be able to do it created a battle of the mind. I couldn't understand why others were doing what I longed to do, but God was not opening the door for me. When your heart's desire is to reach out to others and tell them about Jesus it is hard to wait until the right timing, but God knew exactly what he was doing. Waiting on God to open doors for us when we feel like we know the direction He is leading us is difficult.

In our mind we get discouraged and question, "Why not me?" Looking back, I realize that during those years, I was being prepared for my part in the jail ministry.

Often, I would hear in my spirit the verse, "Study to shew thyself approved unto God, a workman that needeth not to be ashamed, rightly dividing the word of truth." (2 Timothy 2:15 KJV)

Down through the years I have faced many obstacles and adversities, but God has never left me. He has always been faithful love me, guide me, and direct my paths. Through those years, He knew my heart's desire about jail ministry.

I often heard the Lord speak to my heart telling me to pray for the ladies in jail or fast for them. God was preparing and equipping me for the road ahead. I thought I was ready to step into jail ministry when God knew I was not. I felt like I was constantly being put on the potter's wheel.

"Then I went down to the potter's house, and, behold, he wrought a work on the wheels.

4 And the vessel that he made of clay was marred in the hand of the potter: so he made it again another vessel, as seemed good to the potter to make it." (Jeremiah 18:3-4)

It seemed like the more I prayed and fasted, the more Satan aggravated me with troubling thoughts and doubts about myself and about whether God was ever going to open the door for me to be involved in jail ministry.

It became so hard that at one point I became upset and questioned if I could actually endure the wait even though I hadn't made it to even one jail service. It was at that point I realized that I had to sit down and count the cost. No spiritual gift or ministry comes without prayer and fasting. I began to seek the face of the Lord like I never had before. My soul longed to be a part of the jail ministry. I realized that it would be worth whatever God asked me to do to be able to be a part of the ministry.

I would lay in my bed at night and read my Bible and often found myself reading these words:

"Then shall the King say unto them on his right hand, Come, ye blessed of my Father, inherit the kingdom prepared for you from the foundation of the world:

For I was an hungered, and ye gave me meat: I was thirsty, and ye gave me drink: I was a stranger, and ye took me in:

Naked, and ye clothed me: I was sick, and ye visited me: **I was in prison, and ye came unto me.**" (Matthew 34:36)

I started attending a different church several years ago and it wasn't long until a lady in the church approached me. One night she came to me and said, "Hey, you're gonna have to start going with us to the jail to have church with the girls."

She knew nothing about that being my heart's desire over many years. God knew. Needless to say, my heart felt like it was going to burst open with joy! I let her know that I definitely was interested in being involved and couldn't wait to go.

Oh, how my heart rejoiced the first time I walked into the jail! I was scared at first, but I knew my day had come that I had prayed for so many years. The open door to jail ministry came years ago, and at age 55, after all these years of going to the jail, I still feel a little nervous and a lot excited.

I am thrilled to be involved in ministry for God. I'm so thankful I didn't give in to the battles in my mind of fear and doubt about whether God could or would ever let me be part of a women's jail ministry. I'm thankful that I didn't give up and let go of my dream.

Trusting in God for His perfect timing and the right open door is worth the wait.

The LORD is my rock, and my fortress, and my deliverer; my God, my strength, in whom I will trust; my buckler, and the horn of my salvation, and my high tower. (Psalm 18:2 NKJV)

Meet the Authors

Judy Ball
Judy is a widow and a mother of four. She has been involved in church since her childhood, and part of jail ministry outreach for many years.

Clelie Bourne
Clelie is a Newborn Care Specialist who provides loving, experienced care for new mothers and their babies during the first few weeks and months of life. She has assisted over 40 families working with many singletons, twins, triplets and one set of sextuplets.

Brenda Boyens Correll
Brenda was born and raised in South Africa. She loves interacting and gleaning from different cultures, traveling, reading and re-discovering life through the eyes of her kids. She, and her husband love ministering to Christians who are especially in need of help and encouragement to break free and live victorious lives.

Shirley Denton
Shirley was born in Powell County Kentucky. God gave her the gift of writing after the death of her children and empowered her as a woman to witness to His greatness.

Karen Bruce Gross

Karen is a retired social worker at Harlan Appalachain Regional Hospital. Since, she has devoted herself to the Children's program, youth group, and Sunday School youth in her local church and is active in Women's ministry and outreach.

Karen Hall Gross

Karen grew up in Pound, Virginia and attended Bible school at the encouragement of her pastor. She is a retired missionary who spent her career as a Bible Story Teacher working in local schools, churches, and the community. She remains active in her local church ministry programs.

Judith Victoria Hensley

Judith is a retired teacher. She has written a local weekly newspaper column for over twenty years and is the author of many books. She says that in whatever she does, her desire is to obey God's call on her life in that season.

Carol Burgess Johnson

Carol is a retired secretary of East Tennessee State University. She ministers in music as a pianist and soloist. Her call to music ministry began as a child when she first began playing the piano. She serves in her local church and has served on the mission field.

Juanita Lee

Juanita is a cancer survivor. She has filled the role of mother to child, niece, nephew, grandchildren, and foster children, as well as caregiver to her mother. She has a special compassion to care for children who have been abused and/or neglected. For over 25 years, she has also provided volunteer service at the nursing home.

Samantha Martin

Samantha is an administrative secretary who has worked for a variety of companies in the Chicago area. She loves to travel. She is active in her local church and has traveled on mission trips to Honduras and Guatemala.

Geraldine Middleton

Geraldine worked as a nurse at the Harlan Appalachian Regional Hospital where she had the opportunity to share her faith with many patients. She was known as the "singing nurse" She has served as a Sunday school teacher for many years and rejoices in the many miracles she has seen performed by God.

Victoria Odundo

Victoria is the director of Victorious Children's Home in Handidi – Kakamega, Kenya. Through her ministry, she is mother to hundreds of displaced and orphaned children.

Donna Price
Donna Price is a child care provider. She is a pianist, Sunday school teacher, and works with the youth. She is also involved in community outreach.

Rhonda Long Robinson
Rhonda is a former art teacher at the local high school. She has established her own counseling services, known as Day Spring Counseling. Most recently she has joined the staff of Lincoln Memorial University.

Karen Rode
Karen is a retired home schooler/Montessori teacher in upstate New York. Karen is a traveler and adventurer who finds the joy and sees the humor in everyday life.

SLP
SLP is currently working as a Production Manager in the residential Mortgage industry. Forgetting what is behind she is pressing toward the upward call of a life completed as a Servant of the Most High God.

Barb Saylor
Barb is a former department manager at Walmart. Currently, she is a homemaker, a singer, and is active in her local church. She is also involved in community activities.

Flo Shell

Flo is a retired elementary school teacher, who also taught in the education program at Lincoln Memorial University in Harrogate, Tennessee. A widow, she continues to serve in her local church and community, reaching out to those in need.

Darla Shepherd

Darla is coordinator of the local Kentucky Homeplace Office. She is also Director of Ladies' Ministries in her local church and involved in many aspects of ministry.

My flesh and my heart may fail, But God is the strength of my heart and my portion forever. (Psalm 73:26)

Photo Gallery

Lori Bryson   Pages: 26, 64, 137

Sarah Boggs Conatser   Pages: 12, 230, 244

Brenda Boyens Correll   Pages: 25, 210

Debbie Locke-Daniels   Pages: 44, 118, 151

Heather Ealy   Pages: 142, 204

Sheralin Greene   Pages: 128, 249

Patricia Halcomb   Pages: 141, 169, 212

Gladys Hensley   Page: 104

Judith Victoria Hensley   Pages: 24, 136, 229

Judy Saylor Hensley   Page: 10

Kaitlyn Hensley   Page: 11

Kelli Hensley   Pages: 97, 179, 236

Carol Burgess Johnson   Page: 74

Juanita Lee   Page: 32

Victoria Odundo   Page 85

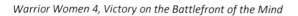

Made in the USA
Middletown, DE
16 October 2018